The 20th Century's MOST INFLUENTIAL HISPANICS

Rigoberta Menchú
Indian Rights Activist

by Stuart A. Kallen

LUCENT BOOKS

An imprint of Thomson Gale, a part of The Thomson Corporation

THOMSON
™
GALE

Detroit • New York • San Francisco • New Haven, Conn. • Waterville, Maine • London

LIBRARY OF CONGRESS CATALOGING-IN-PUBLICATION DATA

Kallen, Stuart A., 1955–
  Rigoberta Menchú, Indian rights activist / by Stuart A. Kallen.
    p. cm. — (The 20th century's most influential Hispanics)
  Includes bibliographical references and index.
  Contents: The story of poor Guatemalans—A young activist—Escape from Guatemala—Telling her story to the world—The Nobel laureate.
  ISBN-13: 978-1-59018-975-7 (hardcover : alk. paper)
  ISBN-10: 1-59018-975-2 (hardcover : alk. paper)
  1. Menchú, Rigoberta—Juvenile literature. 2. Quiché women—Biography—Juvenile literature. 3. Women human rights workers—Biography—Juvenile literature. 4. Mayas—Civil rights—Juvenile literature. 5. Mayas—Government relations—Juvenile literature. 6. Guatemala—Politics and government—Juvenile literature. 7. Guatemala—Ethnic relations—Juvenile literature. I. Title.

  F1465.2.Q5M365 2007
  305.80097281—dc22
  [B]
                                                                    2006025690

Table of Contents

Foreword

When Alberto Gonzales was a boy living in Texas, he never dreamed he would one day stand next to the president of the United States. Born to poor migrant workers, Gonzales grew up in a two-bedroom house shared by his family of ten. There was no telephone or hot water. Because his parents were too poor to send him to college, Gonzales joined the Air Force, but after two years obtained an appointment to the Air Force Academy and, from there, transferred to Rice University. College was still a time of struggle for Gonzales, who had to sell refreshments in the bleachers during football games to support himself. But he eventually went on to Harvard Law School and rose to prominence in the Texas government. And then one day, decades after rising from his humble beginnings in Texas, he found himself standing next to President George W. Bush at the White House. The president had nominated him to be the nation's first Hispanic attorney general. As he accepted the nomination, Gonzales embraced the president and said, "'Just give me a chance to prove myself—that is a common prayer for those in my community. Mr. President, thank you for that chance."

Like Gonzales, many Hispanics in America and elsewhere have shed humble beginnings to soar to impressive and previously unreachable heights. In the twenty-first century, influential Hispanic figures can be found worldwide and in all fields of endeavor including science, politics, education, the arts, sports, religion, and literature. Some accomplishments, like those of musician Carlos Santana or author Alisa Valdes-Rodriguez, have added a much-needed Hispanic voice to the artistic landscape. Others, such as revolutionary Che Guevara or labor leader Dolores Huerta, have spawned international social movements that have enriched the rights of all peoples.

But who exactly is Hispanic? When studying influential Hispanics, it is important to understand what the term actually means. Unlike strictly racial categories like "black" or "Asian," the term "Hispanic" joins a huge swath of people from different countries, religions, and races. The category was first used by the U.S. census bureau in 1980 and is used to refer to Spanish-speaking people of any race. Officially, it denotes a person whose ancestry either descends in whole or in part from the people of Spain or from the various peoples of Spanish-speaking Latin America. Often the term "Hispanic" is used synonymously with the term "Latino," but the two actually have slightly different meanings. "Latino" refers only to people from the countries of Latin America, such as Argentina, Brazil, and Venezuela, whether they speak Spanish or Portuguese. Meanwhile, Hispanic refers only to Spanish-speaking peoples but from any Spanish-speaking country, such as Spain, Puerto Rico, or Mexico.

In America, Hispanics are reaching new heights of cultural influence, buying power, and political clout. More than 35 million people identified themselves as Hispanic on the 2000 U.S. census, and there were estimated to be more than 41 million Hispanics in America as of 2006. In the twenty-first century people of Hispanic origin have officially become the nation's largest ethnic minority, outnumbering both blacks and Asians. Hispanics constitute about 13 percent of the nation's total population, and by 2050 their numbers are expected to rise to 102.6 million, at which point they would account for 24 percent of the total population. With growing numbers and expanding influence, Hispanic leaders, artists, politicians, and scientists in America and in other countries are commanding attention like never before.

These unique and fascinating stories are the subjects of *The Twentieth Century's Most Influential Hispanics* collection from Lucent Books. Each volume in the series critically examines the challenges, accomplishments, and legacy of influential Hispanic figures; many of whom, like Alberto Gonzales, sprang from modest beginnings to achieve groundbreaking goals. *The Twentieth Century's Most Influential Hispanics* offers vivid narrative, fully documented primary and secondary source quotes, a bibliography, thorough index, and mix of color and black and white photographs which enhance each volume and provide excellent starting points for research and discussion.

Introduction

A Struggle to Survive

Rigoberta Menchú Tum, who was awarded the Nobel Peace Prize in 1992, was an unlikely winner of the prestigious honor, which is most often bestowed upon presidents, prime ministers, or religious figures such as as Mother Teresa. In contrast with these dignitaries, Menchú, an indigenous Quiché Maya Indian from Guatemala, spent most of her early life in obscurity and poverty. Her existence was a constant struggle as she and her family toiled on large coffee plantations for extremely low wages.

As a young adult, tired of working as a virtual slave for some of Guatemala's wealthiest landowners, Menchú along with her family members became politically active in an attempt to improve living conditions for the Maya people. In the volatile milieu of Guatemalan society, this made them targets for military authorities. In the years that followed, members of Menchú's family were arrested, viciously tortured, and murdered by government forces.

Menchú, who originally spoke only her traditional Mayan language, learned Spanish in her late teens to tell the world the story of her life, her family, her people, and her struggle. In 1983 this story was published in the book *I, Rigoberta Menchú:*

An Indian Woman in Guatemala. The book became required reading for women's studies, Latin American studies, and other multicultural curricula. Eventually *I, Rigoberta Menchú* was translated into fourteen languages. Nine years after its publication, Menchú won the Nobel Peace Prize.

Menchú's struggle is perhaps even more amazing because millions of Guatemalan peasants fought similar battles for decades—and few outside that small nation paid attention. As Angharad N. Valdivia writes in *A Latina in the Land of Hollywood,* "Many such as she are born, struggle, voice [their protests], resist, and die of natural or artificial causes without ever entering [the international] discourse."[1]

Guatemalan activist Rigoberta Menchú's 1983 autobiography became required reading in many North American universities.

Ancient Mayan ruins still dot the Guatemalan landscape. Menchú's Mayan ancestors built some of the world's most magnificent temples and pyramids.

Maintaining Mayan Customs

The life of the Maya in Guatemala was not always one of travail and protest. Menchú can trace her heritage back more than two thousand years, to a time when Maya civilization flourished throughout Guatemala and the surrounding region. Between approximately 400 B.C. and A.D. 900, Menchú's ancestors built some of the most magnificent ancient pyramids and temples ever constructed in the Western Hemisphere. In addition, the Maya constructed royal palaces, government buildings, and monuments covered with sculpture and intricate picture writing called hieroglyphs. They also developed a system of wells, canals, and reservoirs that provided drinking water for all. By the time the Spanish conquistadors came to the region in 1517, the Maya had constructed a total of two hundred cities connected by grand highways.

The arrival of the Spanish signaled an end to traditional Mayan civilization. Ninety percent of the 10 to 15 million indigenous Maya who inhabited Guatemala were wiped out by war, enslavement, and diseases such as smallpox that the Spanish carried. However, as T. Patrick Culbert writes in *Maya Civilization:*

> The descendants of [the] ancient Maya continue to live in . . . the mountainous areas of Guatemala. . . . [The] Maya of today—village people, supporting themselves mainly by age-old farming systems—continue to speak Maya languages and dress daily in traditional costumes. At ceremonies, the flute and drum sound, incense from the copal tree fills the air, and the names of the ancient gods are chanted (although nowadays intermingled with those of Christian saints). Like ethnic minorities elsewhere around the world, the Maya are under pressure from the dominant culture in their area; still on the margin of the economic and political systems . . . they must struggle to maintain their lands and customs.[2]

The struggles have been severe because although about half the Guatemalan population is indigenous Maya, a higher percentage than in any other Central American country, 70 percent of the nation's agricultural land is controlled by a few extremely wealthy families of Spanish heritage, who represent only about 2 percent of the population. The agricultural system controlled by those families was compared to slavery in a 1986 United Nations report because the daily wage of farmworkers was the equivalent of about $1.75 today. In 2004 the average daily wage for these workers was little more than $3.24. Unable to feed themselves and their families on these low wages, peasants borrow money from the landowner, called a contractor, to pay for corn and beans that they plant on tiny plots of land. After planting their crops, the peasants must work for a fixed period on a finca—a coffee, fruit, or sugarcane plantation—to repay their debt to the contractor. The amount of the loan, plus interest, is automatically deducted from their wages.

When they are not working, Maya are housed in groups of fifty or more in large barnlike structures that have dirt floors and no furniture. Every day the people are provided with small portions of corn and beans, for which they are charged exorbitant prices that increase their debt to the contractor.

The Guatemalan finca system traps workers in a never-ending cycle of poverty that often has dire consequences for young children. Menchú describes some of the tragedies:

> Most of the women who work picking cotton and cof-
> fee, or sometimes cane, have nine or ten children with
> them. Of these, three or four will be more or less
> healthy, and can survive, but most of them have bel-

Malnourished Guatemalan children receive food relief.

lies swollen from malnutrition and the mother knows that four or five of her children could die. We'd been on the *finca* for fifteen days when one of my brothers died from malnutrition. My mother had to miss some days' work to bury him. Two of my brothers died in the *finca*. The first, he was the eldest, was called Felipe. I never knew him. He died when my mother started working. They'd sprayed the coffee with pesticide by plane while we were working, as they usually did, and my brother couldn't stand the fumes and died of poisoning.[3]

Situations such as these, repeated daily throughout Guatemala, created widespread discontent for many decades. Because the government supported the finca system, peasants tried to organize unions and political groups, which were violently repressed by military authorities. This fueled the longest armed conflict in Central American history, a civil war that lasted from 1960 to 1996. In a nation of about 10 million people, the war destroyed more than four hundred villages, created over a million refugees, and left more than two hundred thousand people dead and another forty-five thousand "disappeared,"or kidnapped by government forces and presumed dead. As Larry Habegger and Natanya Pearlman write in *Travelers' Tales Central America*, "The vast majority of the victims were indigenous [Maya], leading some to call the war a campaign of genocide against the civilian population."[4] It was within this environment of misery and bloodshed that Rigoberta Menchú was born and raised. The fact that she, a humble indigenous farmworker, was able to rise to the status of Nobel laureate makes her a unique historical figure. It is little wonder that she is a national hero to many Guatemalans and to millions of others throughout the world.

Chapter 1

The Story of Poor Guatemalans

Rigoberta Menchú Tum is known throughout the world as an activist for indigenous rights, a best-selling author, and a Nobel laureate. However, until she was nearly twenty, Menchú lived in a nation where her worth was largely measured in how many pounds of coffee or cotton she could pick in a day. In the rigidly segregated Guatemalan society, Menchú and millions of indigenous Maya like her lived an existence of hunger, poverty, and sickness. Nonetheless, as the international human rights organization Global Exchange states on its Web site:

> The Mayans have not accepted their fate lightly. A study of their history shows that in every generation since the invasion of the Spaniards [in the 1500s], the Mayans have risen up in rebellion, armed only with rocks and machetes. Every generation, these slave revolts have been quickly crushed by the well armed forces of the oligarchy.[5]

Members of Menchú's generation, like their ancestors, also faced heavily armed soldiers with whatever modest weapons they could assemble. However, Menchú grew up during a time of unprecedented political turmoil, repression, and revolution. And it is within that context that she was transformed from an anonymous farmworker in a rural village to an international spokeswoman for indigenous rights.

Communists and Coups

When Menchú was born on January 9, 1959, the political institutions and people of Guatemala were in a state of chaos. Since the mid-1950s Guatemalan politics had been violently divided

A Mayan boy carries a wreath in a funeral procession for relatives killed in Guatemala's civil war.

between leftist land reformers and right-wing military authorities. Those who supported the leftists were largely poor indigenous Maya. Those on the right were nonindigenous businessmen and landowners of Spanish or mixed-race descent, referred to by the indigenous people as ladinos.

The roots of Guatemala's political division could be traced to 1951, when the left-leaning Jacobo Arbenz Guzmán was elected president by popular vote. Arbenz instituted a series of reforms such as permitting free speech and legalizing unions. To help end starvation among the rural poor, the Arbenz government forced major landholders to sell farmland lying fallow. The expropriated property was then resold at low rates to peasant farming cooperatives. To set an example, Arbenz sold a portion of his own lands.

Although peasants cheered the reforms, the leftist movement in Guatemala had larger implications. Arbenz was elected during the Cold War, a period of intense economic and geopolitical struggles between the United States and the Communist Soviet Union. Small nations such as Guatemala became battlegrounds between communism and capitalism, with peasants and landowners caught up in the ideological conflict.

Power Play

In this tense atmosphere, Arbenz made a series of decisions that disturbed powerful men within the United States government. In 1952 the Guatemalan president granted official recognition to the Communist-backed Labor Party. He also allowed Communists to control important peasant organizations and labor unions and hold several key government positions. In addition, a large percentage of the lands Arbenz expropriated belonged to the powerful United Fruit Company (UFCO), an American corporation that held a near monopoly on fruit production in Guatemala. The company also owned nearly 100 percent of Guatemala's rail lines and shipping facilities.

The U.S. secretary of state, John Foster Dulles, was the head of a law firm that represented the UFCO. His brother, Allen Dulles, was the director of the Central Intelligence Agency (CIA). Both men were fierce anti-Communists who feared Guatemala might be falling under the influence of the Soviet Union. Together, the

"A Spectacular Form of Violence"

Between 1954 and 1996 Guatemalan military regimes conducted a brutal campaign of violence against all political opposition, often with the help of money, weapons, and training from the United States. In 1976 a centrist Guatemalan politician, René de Léon Schlotter, described the conditions in his country in testimony before the United States Congress:

> Guatemala has suffered a spectacular form of violence: spectacular . . . for its intensity—the high number of victims and the cruelty of the methods used.
>
> One of the characteristics of violence in my country is that it . . . is political, carried out for political reasons: the establishment of terror for the general purpose of eliminating an adversary. Another feature of this phenomenon is that it is mainly from the right. . . . [Groups] of the extreme right have used violence as their only tool.
>
> The violence organized by these groups has a double purpose: first to sow terror and bring people to their knees in fear of their lives . . . [and] second to eliminate opponents. . . . In Guatemala . . . they don't bother with detention: the opponent is killed or "kidnapped" in the streets and just disappears. . . . With its policy of military and police assistance, the United States has collaborated in the acts of repression, and consequently the violation of human rights.

Quoted in Stephen Schlesinger and Stephen Kinzer, *Bitter Fruit.* Cambridge, MA: Harvard University, 1999, pp. 250–51.

Remains of Guatemalan massacre victims await identification.

Dulles brothers worked with CIA operatives to bring about a coup that replaced Arbenz with Carlos Castillo Armas, a colonel in the Guatemalan army. The expropriated lands were returned to the UFCO and other landowners. Global Exchange explains what followed:

> A bloodbath ensued, peasant cooperatives were destroyed, unions and political parties crushed, and dissidents hunted down. Thousands were killed and many more fled the country. Recently released CIA documents include a CIA hit list prepared before the coup, identifying political and intellectual leaders as military targets. A military dictatorship was installed in the presidency and remained there until 1986.[6]

After the military coup dislodged the Communist government, Guatemala remained extremely unstable. The year before Menchú was born, Castillo was murdered by men working for General Michael Ydigoras Fuentes, who was then named president. Two years later, a group of junior military officers who had once backed Arbenz organized a coup against Ydigoras. When the takeover failed, the plotters formed several left-wing guerrilla groups that became known by their Spanish acronyms. These included the Guerrilla Army of the Poor (EGP), the Revolutionary Organization of Armed People (ORPA), the Rebel Armed Forces (FAR), and the Guatemalan Labor Party (PGT). During the next thirty-six years these groups and others engaged in a civil war in Guatemala, conducting economic sabotage, targeting government installations, and fighting members of government security forces.

A Famous Leader

Rigoberta Menchú is the most famous indigenous leader in the world.

Mary Louise Pratt, quoted in Arturo Arias, ed., *The Rigoberta Menchú Controversy.* Minneapolis: University of Minnesota Press, 2001, p. 29.

In response, the Guatemalan government formed right-wing paramilitary death squads such as the National Organized Anti-

Communist Movement (MANO) and Eye for an Eye (OJO). According to scholar Daniel L. Premo, these groups murdered both centrist supporters of Arbenz and anyone remotely associated with the guerrilla groups:

> [Under] the cover of anti-guerrilla activity, non-communist leftists were sought out by right-wing terror groups and eliminated. Leaflets appeared threatening . . . students, intellectuals, trade unionists, and professional people who sought to organize or protest against what they considered social injustice. Between October 1966 and March 1968 an estimated 3,000 to 8,000 Guatemalans were killed in [paramilitary] campaigns.[7]

The practices institutionalized by these government security forces—kidnapping, torture, and execution of political activists—would eventually come to play a large role in the life of Rigoberta Menchú. So too would Guatemala's lack of land reforms, indigenous rights, and political freedom. However, when Menchú was young, most of the violence was taking place far away from her in the nation's capital, Guatemala City. In the rural department, or state, where the Menchús lived, the fight was not a battle over political ideology but a struggle to obtain the basic necessities of life.

"Practically a Paradise"

In the early years of her life, Menchú lived for four months of the year in the department of Quiché, named after her tribe. As a Quiché Indian, Menchú belonged to one of twenty-two indigenous groups in Guatemala, each with its own customs and language. Menchú considers the Spanish-speaking ladinos who dominate business, the government, and the military to be Guatemala's twenty-third ethnic group.

Menchú's home was in an isolated mountainous region she describes as "practically a paradise, the country is so beautiful. There are no big roads, and no cars. Only people can reach it."[8] The nearest town, Chimel, where Menchú was born, is 15 miles (24km) from her family home.

Chimel was a peaceful place in the early 1960s. According to one unnamed resident, "There was a chapel, a school, medical clinics, a soccer team that played with other villages. . . . And the people had their little fiestas; they got together to kill a sheep, a pig, and everyone ate together. . . . Nearly everyone had respect."[9] However, most of the homes that peasants lived in lacked electricity, running water, and sewage disposal.

Menchú's mother, Rosa, and father, Vicente, moved to the Chimel region in 1960. Both came from extremely impoverished backgrounds. Vicente Menchú was an orphan who, as a young man, chopped wood and worked on fincas, earning about thirty cents a day. When there was no corn to eat, he foraged in the jungle for food. After a year of forced service in the Guatemalan military, Menchú met Juana Tum Cotojá, and the two were married.

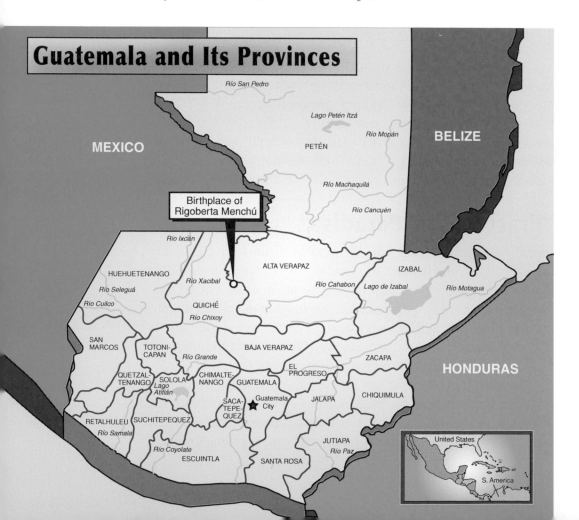

Guatemala and Its Provinces

Although the young couple had little money, they were able to pay the required government fee that allowed them to build a house and clear land to farm. This was extremely difficult work in the cool highland climate, where the soil was rocky and thin. With six children to feed, the Menchús tried to keep chickens and sheep, but the livestock was often killed by wild animals in the surrounding jungle. The family also planted corn, beans, and other crops, but it was about eight years before the fields were productive.

Even after the fields were established, they provided only enough food to last about four months. When this meager harvest was exhausted, the family would plant another crop and leave home, traveling to the fertile coastal regions of Guatemala to work on the fincas.

Life on the Fincas

Life on the fincas was extremely harsh, and simply traveling back and forth was a traumatic experience for Menchú. The transportation to the fincas was provided by the landowner, who packed up to forty men, women, and children into the back of a stiflingly hot lorry, or truck. Riders brought plates, cups, water bottles, and enough clothes to spend several months away from home. Many also brought animals, such as dogs, cats, and chickens, since no one remained behind to care for them. In the 1960s the trip from Chimel to the Pacific coast took about thirty hours, and there were few bathroom breaks. Menchú describes the conditions:

> During the trip the animals and the small children used to dirty the lorry and you'd get people vomiting and wetting themselves. By the end of the journey, the smell—the filth of the people and animals—was unbearable. . . . The lorry is covered with a tarpaulin so you can't see the countryside you're passing through. . . . The stuffiness inside the lorry with the cover on, and the smell . . . makes you want to be sick yourself. . . . By the time we got to the *finca*, we were totally stupefied; we were like chickens coming out of a pot.[10]

Indigenous children work long hours beside their parents in an onion field on a finca in southern Guatemala.

Workers were given little time to recuperate after the harrowing journey. The minute they jumped down from the lorries, machine-gun-toting men, called corporals, began to shout orders. Anyone who offered the slightest resistance was clubbed and beaten. When working the fields, men, women, and children—some as young as four—were closely supervised. Slow workers were punished, and those who tried to rest were threatened with beatings.

During Menchú's early childhood on the fincas, she cared for her younger brothers and sisters while her mother, often with a new-born baby on her back, labored in the fields. At the age of eight, Menchú began working until eight o'clock every night, picking 35 pounds (16k) of coffee a day for about 20 cents. Although the entire family labored from sunup to sundown, their wages were so low that the children starved. Menchú describes the situation: "[My] two eldest brothers [died] from lack of food when we were down on the *fincas*. Most Indian families suffer from malnutrition. Most of them don't even reach fifteen years old. When children are growing and don't get enough to eat, they're often ill, and this . . . well . . . it complicates the situation."[11]

Malnutrition was common because children who were too young to work were given nothing, and parents had to share their already meager portions with them. In addition, the tortillas and beans that were provided were often rotten and did not make for a well-rounded diet. Menchú says that an individual would be given a single egg in a one-month period. Workers could supplement their diets by purchasing foods at contractor-owned cantinas, or stores, that sold alcoholic beverages, soft drinks, canned goods, candy, medicine, and cakes. The prices at these stores were exorbitant, however, and as Menchú explains, kept the workers from earning any money at all: "[Everything] they buy is marked up on an account, and at the end when you get your pay, you always owe

Generations of Guatemalan Mayans have lived in poverty under the finca system.

so much for food, so much at the shop, so much at the pharmacy. You end up owing a lot. . . . They deduct for everything and you end up having to pay debts before you can leave."[12]

Many of the debts incurred by the workers were for necessities such as medicine and water. Young children often became sick from the lack of restroom facilities on fincas, where up to four hundred people might use a long ditch in the forest as a toilet. In addition, contractors rarely provided drinking water, and workers were forced to either buy water or fill bottles from irrigation canals or drainage ditches polluted with pesticides and sewage. Insect bites were also a problem. On occasion, when the Menchús arrived at a finca before work began, they were forced to sleep outdoors. One of Menchú's early memories is of clouds of mosquitoes descending on her family, covering their faces and other exposed flesh with hundred of bites.

Religious Traditions

The Menchús, like many Maya, were sustained through these hardships by their ancient religious beliefs. In her autobiography *I, Rigoberta Menchú: An Indian Woman in Guatemala* Menchú provides many details concerning the traditions that have given her strength and courage over the years. For example, she explains that when she was just a baby, she was given a protective spirit, called a *nahual*, that she believes has followed her throughout her life. Children are not told about their *nahuals* until they are about eleven years old. *Nahuals* are usually represented by plants, natural elements such as fire, and animals such as birds, bulls, dogs, cats, and lions.

When she was twelve years old, Menchú began practicing a second religion: Catholicism, taught by priests who visited Chimel a few times a year. Like many Maya, Menchú combined the Catholic belief of a single God with the concept of *nahuals*.

Because Menchú could neither read nor write, she learned religious texts, prayers, and rosaries by memorization. A good student, Menchú excelled at her lessons and was recruited by the priests to teach younger children. She also worked with other children to raise money for the church through a small village enterprise that sold salt and other necessities.

Mayan villagers, who often mix ancient rituals with Catholicism, prepare for a ceremony honoring civil war dead.

Catholicism became central to Menchú's social life and provided her with a basis for working within the community. This work took on a political aspect when Menchú's best friend, Maria, died after pesticides were sprayed on her while she was working in a cotton field. To protest Maria's death, Menchú joined ten others from her catechism group who refused to work on the finca for two days. Although not a formal strike, the action motivated Menchú to begin questioning the finca system and wondering why her friend, along with her younger brother at an earlier time, were allowed to be poisoned. She even had thoughts about setting fire to the finca so no one else would die there.

After Maria's death Menchú vowed to get away from the fincas. Although she was only eleven years old and had never been alone in Guatemala City, her parents allowed her to move there and work as a maid for a wealthy family. However, the family treated Menchú badly, slapping her, yelling at her, feeding her less than the family dog, and paying her only five dollars a month.

Ancient Traditions

The Mayan people continue to practice their traditional cultural beliefs. In *I, Rigoberta Menchú: An Indian Woman in Guatemala* Rigoberta Menchú describes a ritual performed by pregnant women:

> [When a pregnant woman is] in her seventh month, the mother introduces her baby to the natural world, as our customs tell her to. She goes out in the fields or walks over the hills. She also has to show her baby the kind of life she leads, so that if she gets up at three in the morning, does her chores and tends the animals, she does it all the more so when she's pregnant, conscious that the child is taking all this in. She talks to the child continuously from the first moment he's in her stomach, telling him how hard his life will be. It's as if the mother were a guide explaining things to a tourist. She'll say, for instance: "You must never abuse nature and you must live your life as honestly as I do." As she works in the fields, she tells her child all the little things about her work. It's a duty to her child that a mother must fulfil.

Rigoberta Menchú, *I Rigoberta Menchú: An Indian Woman in Guatemala.* London: Verso, 1983, pp. 7–8.

After enduring constant physical and mental abuse for a year, Menchú returned to Chimel in 1970, only to find that her father had been arrested. Vicente Menchú had been engaged in a legal dispute over a piece of land for nearly a decade, and the government responded by jailing him. This event shocked the family and marked the beginning of Menchu's political awakening.

"The Government Is a Bandit"

Land disputes like the one involving Vicente Menchú are common in Guatemala, where fertile coastal land is very expensive, and the poor are forced to live in the less productive highlands. Many, like the Menchús, survive only as a result of years of backbreaking work, including clearing the jungle and fertilizing fields. Once the crops are growing and the fruit trees are producing, however, peasants sometimes find that a wealthy ladino wants to claim their property. The Indians, most of whom do not understand Spanish, must then deal with ladino mayors, military commissioners, judges, lawyers, and governors in an attempt to keep their property. The odds are against the Maya because many of the officials require bribes, fees, taxes, or payments beyond the means of those who work on the fincas. If the peasants lose their cases, the landowners often allow them to stay on the land, but they must labor for very low wages as they do on the fincas.

A Mayan family harvests coffee beans. Successful native farms were often taken over by ladinos.

A disgruntled peasant awaits relocation after the government confiscated his farm.

The Menchús' land dispute began in 1961. According to Rigoberta, the wealthy García family brought in inspectors and engineers to survey Vicente's land, claiming that it was theirs. Vicente organized meetings in the town, collected money, and implored others to join him in stopping the Garcías. After gathering dozens of signatures, Vicente went to the capital and presented a petition of protest to the Guatemalan National Institute for Agrarian Transformation (INTA), which handled land matters. As was typical in such situations, the government moved very slowly, not responding to the petition for three and a half years. Meanwhile, the Menchús were forced to pay for lawyers, government fees, and surveying teams in order to hold their claim on the land.

The injustice Vicente found in the Guatemalan bureaucracy created extreme frustration, according to an unnamed neighbor: "INTA deceived him many times. It would say the petition had been lost, that his lands needed to be surveyed again. It said that it would deliver his titles and not do it. Trip after trip to the capital. Those people, that man, went through hardships. . . . The government is a bandit because it always takes our money."[13]

The need for repeated surveys of the land created further hardships, as Menchú writes:

> What I can't forgive, and this is something which has contributed to my hate for these people, is that they said they came to help us. My father, mother, all the community, were very distressed. [The engineers] were *ladinos*. They couldn't eat our food, our *tortillas* with salt. If we didn't feed them well they would probably favor the landowners. So we treated them very well, out of fear. We gave them our best, our fattest animals. We'd kill chickens for them to eat. Our community, which never bought so much as a bottle of oil, had to buy them rice, oil, eggs, chickens, meat. We had to buy coffee and sugar. . . . We all had to go to town. The village got together, gave in their ten *centavos* [cents] and with this collection we bought what was needed. Earning ten centavos is hard for us, it's earned by a lot of sweat. It was worse when the inspectors stayed a whole week. When they left, the village breathed a sigh of relief and we were much poorer. *We* didn't eat meat. *They* did.[14]

Menchú claims that this situation repeated itself more than twenty times. Meanwhile, the García family became more aggressive, sending a group of soldiers to evict the villagers. After the peasants were forced to leave, the soldiers pillaged the village, breaking pots and pans, stealing what valuables they could find, and killing the animals. Menchú writes: "Those few days confirmed my hatred for those people. I saw why we said that *ladinos* were thieves, criminals, and liars."[15]

Resistance

Rigoberta Menchú was born into a family grounded in activism for land and indigenous rights. Within the Guatemalan reality, where a politics of indigenous extermination is thinly veiled, surviving becomes an act of resistance.

Angharad N. Valdivia, *A Latina in the Land of Hollywood.* Tucson: University of Arizona Press, 2000, p. 109.

In the following months there were several similar raids as government officials stood by idly. This prompted Vicente Menchú to organize protests against the government not only within his local community but also in nearby villages. He asked the Guatemalan Federation of Independent Unions (FASGUA) to help with his cause. During this time, Rigoberta rarely saw her father, who was constantly traveling to meetings with various villagers, the INTA, and the federation. Recognizing a challenge to their power, the landowners began using their government connections to threaten Vicente. Finally, he was arrested and charged with "compromising the sovereignty . . . and the well-being of Guatemalans."[16] This charge, as serious as treason, called for a prison sentence of eighteen years.

With the arrest of her father, Menchú found her life suddenly changed as she began working extensively with her family to free him. After fifteen months the Menchús were successful, but Rigoberta was no longer a demure peasant girl. With a vision of social justice and a drive to organize that she had inherited from her father, Rigoberta Menchú, although she was only eleven years old, had begun to learn that a single person can make a difference.

Chapter 2

A Young Activist

In September 1970 Rigoberta Menchú's father, Vicente, was arrested in a dispute over land. His imprisonment spurred Rigoberta to organize protests and other actions to free him. Menchú's political awakening took place at a time when the civil war in Guatemala was growing increasingly bloody. By 1970 leftist guerrillas had been largely driven out of the major cities. Hoping to revive their cause, the guerrillas began recruiting the indigenous peasants in the countryside while establishing permanent bases in the jungles that surrounded rural villages.

At the same time, those within the government who opposed the guerrillas were growing stronger. In 1970 rightists elected an army colonel, Carlos Arana Osorio, president. The former commander of the Zacapa military district, Arana Osorio was known as the Jackal of Zacapa for his brutal campaigns against leftists. In *Unfinished Conquest*, Guatemalan journalist Victor Perera explains:

> In October 1966, Colonel Carlos Arana Osorio. . . launched a counterinsurgency campaign with the support of one thousand U.S. Green Berets and vigilante death squadrons composed largely of ranchers

and off-duty police units. The campaign was to cost eight thousand lives in two years, including those of students and professors, labor leaders, and journalists; in the eastern provinces, hundreds of innocent peasants lost their homes and families in Vietnam-style search-and-destroy operations. In 1970 Carlos Arana Osorio . . . [was] elected president and unleashed a second wave of terror against rural and urban

Menchú, who embarked on her political activism as a teenager, takes part in a ceremony honoring victims of genocide.

insurgent movements. The United States once again did its share by training 32,000 Guatemalan policemen. . . . Together with the paramilitary death squadrons that continued to operate in the capital and the countryside, Arana's second pacification campaign accounted for approximately 15,000 killed or disappeared during his first three years in office.[17]

The number of deaths listed by Perera has been confirmed by the United Nations. However, according to human rights watchdog group Amnesty International, there were only about three hundred to five hundred guerrillas operating in Guatemala between 1966 and 1970. Thus, these numbers show that most of those killed did not take up arms against their government. And the mounting death toll radicalized many peasants, including Rigoberta Menchú.

"We Had to Defeat the Enemy"

The military campaigns in rural areas served as a backdrop to the Menchú family's foremost problem: freeing Vicente. To pay fees for lawyers, witnesses, and documents, Menchú again began working every day on the fincas, not returning home for fifteen months. She gave her meager earnings to her brothers who were also working on the fincas. Once a month, one of the boys returned to Chimel to give the money to their mother, who also collected small donations from sympathetic neighbors.

The effort to free Vicente was made more difficult by the fact that the Menchús did not speak Spanish. After paying scarce funds to interpreters, Menchú vowed she would learn Spanish so she could personally deal with government officials in the future.

Although his enemies were alleged to have paid off judges to keep him in prison, Menchú's father was finally freed in mid-1971. The angry landowners vowed to kill him. Despite the threats, Vicente began to travel clandestinely through the countryside to work with union organizers who were trying to improve living and working conditions for the Indians.

In constant fear for her father's life, Menchú came to believe that landowners, soldiers, and the rich in Guatemala were enemies that she must learn to fight. She writes:

We began using the term "enemies," because we didn't have the notion of enemy in our culture, until those people arrived to exploit us, oppress us and discriminate against us. In our community we are all equal. . . . There is no superior or inferior. But we realized that in Guatemala there was something superior and something inferior and that *we* were the inferior. The *ladinos* behave like a superior race. . . . I threw myself into my work and I told myself we had to defeat the enemy."[18]

Menchú and the neighbors who sympathized with her beliefs began to organize against their adversaries. With no money and few weapons, the Indians adopted strategies their ancient ancestors had used against the Spanish conquistadors. For example, the Maya knew they could immobilize a soldier by throwing red pep-

This indigenous family found safe haven from murderous military units by making its home in the Guatemalan jungle.

per or lime into his eyes, so people began to carry these substances in case they were needed. The Maya also began digging deep pits along strategic paths and in front of dwellings. The holes were covered with nets and brush, and any approaching soldier would fall into the trap.

For safety purposes the villagers built communal shelters in the forests, where they could hide away from homes. In addition, they set up security watches to signal villagers when the military was approaching. These signals warned everyone to leave the village and execute emergency evacuation procedures.

The villagers had the chance to test their strategies when Vicente and one of his sons was kidnapped by guards who worked for the landowners. The son got away and ran back to the village, where a mob of peasants, armed with rocks, hoes, machetes, and sticks, formed to fight the guards. When they spotted the mob, the kidnappers escaped. Vicente had been tortured. His scalp had been torn off and his arms, legs, and ribs were broken. He spent nine months in the hospital and never fully recovered from the beating. Although he survived, the incident terrorized the Menchús, who lived under the constant fear that Vicente would be kidnapped once again, tortured, and killed.

The Committee for Peasant Unity

After Vicente was released from the hospital, Menchú began traveling with him for several reasons. She wanted to know where he was at all times in case he was arrested or kidnapped, and she wanted to meet his political contacts so she could carry on his work if he disappeared. At this time the Menchús were raising money from community-based supporters, priests, and sympathetic Europeans who traveled to Guatemala to fight for indigenous rights. During her travels Menchú took Spanish lessons from priests and nuns in various villages and towns.

In 1977 Menchú's father was arrested again and held for fifteen days. After his release, Vicente said he was inspired to join an organization that would "fight the rich because they have become rich with our land, our crops."[19] Acting on this belief, Vicente helped found the Committee for Peasant Unity (CUC) in 1978. The purpose of the group was to provide political representation to all rural workers, as David Stoll explains in *Rigoberta Menchú and the Story of All Poor Guatemalans:* "CUC wanted to bring together different categories of peasants. It wanted to unite rural proletarians [poor working people] and small [landholders], the landless and the land-strapped, ladinos and [Indians]. . . . Starting in 1978, CUC denounced the oligarchy in no uncertain terms. It wanted living wages and the distribution of estates."[20]

With these broad goals, the CUC became the first Guatemalan political movement to link the interests of Indians with those of poor ladinos. However, the group was considered subversive by the government and was forced to operate in secret. In order to spare his family any danger, Vicente moved away from home after he joined the CUC, living in clandestine mountain bases and visiting his wife and children only late at night.

Despite its shadowy existence the CUC was able to enlist a growing number of peasants. Traveling from village to village, organizers gave speeches to Maya laborers calling upon them to organize and insist upon civil rights. The CUC had a list of demands that included raising the daily wage from 1.20 quetzals (about 75 cents in U.S. dollars in 2006) to a minimum of 3.20 quetzals (about 2.00 dollars). In addition, the CUC appealed for safer working conditions, especially pertaining to the careless use of pesticides. At the time, cotton farmers were spraying the extremely toxic pesticide DDT at levels four times higher than those considered safe. Field workers were dying of lung and liver ailments, and the breast milk of indigenous mothers had the highest concentration of DDT in the Western Hemisphere.

"People, Not Animals"

In the summer of 1978 the CUC found another, more urgent, cause to support. The trouble began in May, when the Guatemalan government evicted eight hundred Keckchi Indians from their homes in the town of Panzós in the north-central part of Guatemala. The property was expropriated because oil had been discovered there and the drilling rights had been sold to a Canadian company. On May 29 the displaced Indians, with nowhere to go, marched into the Panzós town square where they were met by dozens of soldiers. Author Greg Grandin describes the situation:

At a ceremony, a Mayan widow carries a photo of her murdered husband.

What happened next has been disputed. Some say that the protesters were peaceful and that soldiers stationed in the square opened fire in order to eliminate the leaders of the land movement. Others say that they provoked the soldiers by throwing chili powder in their eyes, threatening them with sticks, and demanding the installation of a "Mayan king" to head the republic.[21]

Panzós villagers commemorate the victims of a 1978 government massacre of Indian protesters.

Whatever the reason, the soldiers fired upon the crowd, killing thirty-five men, women, and children, and wounding forty-seven. Another eighteen people drowned in the Polochic River while attempting to escape.

The massacre in Panzós elicited widespread public outcry. On June 1 and June 8, thousands of unionists and students, led by the CUC, took to the streets in the capital to protest the violence. In addition, the CUC bought newspaper and radio ads that denounced the slaughter and called for all the workers in the countryside to unite against government repression. Because the CUC was dedicated to creating an all-inclusive, multiethnic organization, the murdered Keckchis were not referred to as Indians, but simply as honest workers from rural areas.

Joining the CUC

Frustrated by the abuses perpetrated by the government, Rigoberta joined the CUC around the time of her twentieth birthday in January 1979. Her job was to work as a community organizer, laboring on fincas while secretly recruiting workers to join the CUC.

One of the early campaigns Menchú worked on involved a challenge to the practices of the Guatemalan Forestry Commission (INAFOR), a national agency that managed tree harvests. The INAFOR was set up in 1975 to regulate logging by collecting a fee of five quetzals for every tree that was cut on public lands. Anyone who wanted to cut trees had to petition a judge, in Spanish, for permission. Those who ignored the law could be arrested, beaten, and imprisoned.

This was a particularly onerous situation for most indigenous Guatemalans, who relied on wood for cooking and heating. In addition, the charge per tree amounted to several days' wages. Major landowners, by contrast, had no problems paying the fees and were thus free to cut down hundreds of acres of forest for export, leaving nearby villages with no source of energy.

Menchú organized a campaign respectfully requesting the unrestricted right to cut trees as Indians had in the past, but the government refused. Without access to wood, many peasants were forced to leave their rural villages and go to the coasts, where they hoped to work on the fincas.

Suffering

She suffered greatly seeing her whole family dispersed by the violence.

Clemente Díaz Cano, quoted in Larry Rohter, "Tarnished Laureate," *New York Times*, December 15, 1998, p. 1.

The INAFOR policy that displaced thousands of rural Maya was extremely beneficial to the landowners. The flood of willing workers allowed them to further depress wages and cut back on food rations. Those who protested were immediately fired and replaced by one of the countless hungry, unemployed peasants willing to work without complaint. Such policies created a backlash, however, and helped provide the CUC with hundreds of new recruits. As a result of the group's growing power, its leaders decided to petition the government for official recognition as a union that represented the peasants. Menchú writes: "Our objectives were: a fair wage from the landowners; respect for our communities; the decent treatment we deserve as people, not animals; respect for our religion, our customs, and our culture."[22] As was so often the case, the group received no reply to their petition.

Befriending Ladinos

As one of the leading activists in the CUC, Menchú began to recognize the benefits of recruiting poor ladino peasants, who also lived in dire circumstances. Although she had previously thought of all ladinos as enemies, her attitude began to change when she befriended an unnamed middle-class ladino intellectual and CUC member who helped her with her Spanish lessons. Referring to him as her *compañero*, or companion, Menchú writes:

> That *compañero* taught me many things, one of which was to love *ladinos* a lot. He taught me to think more clearly about some of my ideas which were wrong, like saying all *ladinos* are bad. He didn't teach me through ideas, he showed me by his actions, by the way he behaved towards me. . . . [The] example of my *compañero ladino* made me really understand the barrier which has been put up between the Indian and the *ladino*, and that because of this same system which tries to divide us, we haven't understood that *ladinos* also live in terrible conditions, same as we do. . . . All our country's riches are in the hands of a few.[23]

Working with her *compañero*, Menchú traveled among people of many backgrounds who were sympathetic to her cause. She listened to ideas and complaints at a local level and passed them up the chain of CUC command. The matters were first considered by

Rejecting Discrimination

Because of painful experiences with discrimination, Rigoberta Menchú developed an intense dislike of ladinos. However, as she gained increasing responsibilities as an organizer for the Committee for Peasant Unity (CUC), her attitudes towards her *compañeros* ladinos, or ladino companions, changed. As she explains in *I, Rigoberta Menchú*:

> Discrimination had made me isolate myself completely from the world of our *compañeros ladinos*. I didn't express certain of my attitudes but they were nevertheless there, like a thorn in my heart, from having been repeated so many times. "They are *ladinos*, they can't understand because they are *ladinos*." But slowly, through our discussions, we understood each other. . . . To bring about change we had to unite, Indians and *ladinos*. What they valued most in me was my knowledge of self-defense, my knowledge of our traps, and escape routes. I could teach other *compañeros*. And later on, through my involvement in the struggle—through my participation as a woman, as a Christian, and as an Indian—I was given responsibilities which recognized my abilities as well. So I had a lot of responsibility. . . . I was by now an educated woman. . . . I knew the history of my people, and the history of my *compañeros* from other ethnic groups.

Rigoberta Menchú, *I, Rigoberta Menchú*. London: Verso, 1983, pp.168–69.

a regional group and then given to the national coordinating body for the CUC. This work brought Menchú into close contact with hundreds of activists she began to call her *compañeros* ladinos.

Yet despite CUC's attempt to recruit them, not all poor ladinos empathized with the Indians. Many felt that no matter how poor they were, they still held an advantage over the Maya in Guatemalan society. Menchú explains: "[Between] these poor *ladinos* and Indians there is still that big barrier. No matter how bad their conditions are, they feel *ladino*, and being *ladino* is something important in itself; it's *not* being an Indian. . . . [Even] though the *ladino* is poor, even though he's exploited as we are, he tries to be something better than the Indian."[24]

Guerrilla Army of the Poor

There was another reason that some ladinos were reluctant to join Menchú's organization. It was an open secret that CUC was collaborating with the Guerrilla Army of the Poor (EGP), a Marxist organization that advocated the overthrow of the Guatemalan government. Only the most committed revolutionaries were willing to risk the government's wrath by supporting the EGP.

Despite the perils of membership, however, in 1979 EGP was the largest guerrilla army in Guatemala, having first established a presence among the indigenous communities in Quiché in the mid-1970s. After joining forces with the CUC, one of the largest peasant organizations, members of the EGP were able to shape the political positions of Menchú's group and take their Marxist message to a wider segment of society. They believed that all means of production, such as farms and factories, should be communally owned. They also

Indian leaders stack up brightly-colored coffins holding the remains of those killed by Guatemalan soldiers in 1982.

believed that society should be classless, that there should be no social groups with greater status, privilege, or authority than others.

The Marxist influence of the EGP on the CUC may be seen in statements such as the one put out by a propaganda arm of the group, called the Compañeros of CUC, in the early 1980s:

> CUC was born for war. From the beginning, issues were raised which implied a profound, structural, revolutionary change. We can say, then, that the strategic objective of the organization is to prepare the masses for insurrectional opportunities, for the final stages of popular war. . . . [CUC] is a revolutionary organization of peasant masses.[25]

Such pronouncements alarmed Guatemala's military dictators, especially as the influence of the CUC grew among Guatemalan peasants, who were joining the group for several reasons. Some people were threatened by armed insurgents who forced them to cooperate. Others who would have preferred to remain neutral were forced to choose sides under pressure from neighbors, guerrillas, or government forces. Finally, there were those like the Menchús, who adopted extremist philosophies because of their desperation, described by Perera as resulting from "the subhuman pay scale on the fincas, the rape of workers' wives by landowners, [and] the extortions by [contractors] who created a vicious cycle of indebted labor through a variety of devious schemes and entrapments."[26]

The growing support for the CUC created an unprecedented government backlash after Romeo Lucas García was elected president of Guatemala in 1978. According to Perera, Lucas García "unleashed the most ruthless repression against Mayas in Guatemala's long history of repressive military dictatorships."[27] Lucas García set up military bases in rural areas so that soldiers, many of them Indians themselves who were forced into military service, could institute a terror campaign of rape, kidnapping, torture, and murder against the indigenous Maya. In the months that followed, leaders of leftist political groups were abducted, tied up in sacks, flown high above the Pacific Ocean in helicopters, and pushed to their deaths in the sea. Hundreds of less important activists were shot or hacked to death with machetes, their bodies dumped on roadsides. In many instances Indians walking in the forests might find thirty or forty mutilated bodies being fed upon by insects and wild animals.

The Torture of Brother Petrocinio

As the Guatemalan civil war escalated, the number of strikes, protest marches, and revolutionary pronouncements increased. During this time, Menchú continued to travel throughout the countryside, talking with sympathizers and sleeping in a different house every night to avoid arrest. Menchú's youngest brother, sixteen-year-old Petrocinio, was also active in organizing, but unlike his sister remained close to Chimel. On September 9, 1979, one of Petrocinio's neighbors turned him in to military authorities for a reward of about fifteen dollars. During the next sixteen days, Petrocinio was gruesomely tortured while being interrogated about guerrilla activities. His fingers were cut off, his scalp was slit and pulled down over his face, his genitals were mutilated, and he was burned.

After learning of Petrocinio's disappearance, Vicente Menchú returned to his village. Soon thereafter, in a bizarre spectacle, military leaders forced villagers, including Menchú's parents, to assemble in the town square. Surrounded by hundreds of heavily armed soldiers, dozens of dazed, barely alive torture victims, including Petrocinio, were brought forth and dragged before the assembled peasants. As family members wept, a general lectured the Indians about the evils of communism and warned that anyone who joined the guerrilla movement would face the same fate as the prisoners. Menchú describes the horrific scene:

> My mother was weeping; she was looking at her son. My brother scarcely recognized us. . . . My mother said he did, that he could still smile at her. . . . [The victims] were monstrous. They were all fat, fat, fat. They were all swollen up, all wounded. . . . Somewhere around halfway through the speech, it would be about an hour and a half, two hours on, the captain made the squad of soldiers take the clothes off the tortured people, saying that it was so that everyone could see for themselves what their punishment had been and realize that if we

A Soldier Speaks

Many soldiers who carried out atrocities against the Maya were young indigenous men themselves. They were often forced to enter the military and carry out orders under the penalty of torture or death. One such soldier, Chilin Hultaxh, a Quiché Indian, describes his experience in the Guatemalan army:

> Many of our indigenous brothers are captured for military service; they are terrified and run away, which the army considers an act of high treason. These cases are punishable by death. In times of war martial law demands that deserters be shot on the spot. The soldier who doesn't follow orders from superiors gets punished severely. Sentences range from prison to the dungeon, which is a pit filled with filthy water that has human waste, food leftovers, and other disgusting stuff floating in it. Into the pit they throw soldiers who have transgressed or been disobedient. They leave them there for a day or a night. We know that in Huehuetenango two soldiers died that way. . . . It's a type of torture given to the indigenous soldier to convince him that he should follow orders blindly. It instills fear.

Quoted in Victor Montejo, *Voices from Exile: Violence and Survival in Modern Maya History.* Norman: University of Oklahoma Press, 1999, p. 89.

The government forced native peasants like these to fight their own people.

got mixed up in communism, in terrorism, we'd be punished the same way. . . . They couldn't simply take the clothes off the tortured men, so the soldiers brought scissors and cut the clothes apart from the feet up and took the clothes off the tortured bodies. They all had the marks of different tortures. The captain devoted himself to explaining each of the different tortures. This is perforation with needles, he'd say, this is a wire burn. He went on like that explaining each torture and describing each tortured man.[28]

In a final ghastly act, the soldiers poured gasoline over the victims and set them on fire. This finally enraged the crowd to the point that they rushed at the soldiers, waving machetes over their heads. The soldiers retreated to their trucks and drove off, shouting nationalistic slogans.

Wordless Admiration

Rigoberta's presentation left most of us stunned and filled with wordless admiration. . . . [Her] subdued matter-of-fact delivery magnified the horror of the events she described, without sensationalizing them.

Victor Perera, *Unfinished Conquest*. Berkeley and Los Angeles: University of California, 1993, pp. 319–20.

Grisly scenes like the one in Chimel were repeated in countless villages throughout Guatemala in the 1980s. As Perera writes, "Rigoberta Menchú's testimony is entirely consistent with other eyewitness accounts of torture, burnings, and mass executions that I have gathered myself."[29] In the following years, government supporters argued that the Communist threat to Guatemala warranted such behavior. However, the United Nations has issued several reports calling these incidents war crimes. In addition, such measures served only to impel the Indians to join the guerrillas. Victor Menchú was one example. Enraged by Petrocinio's death, he joined the EGP. Rigoberta went back to her CUC activities, more dedicated than ever to ending the military dictatorship that was causing such intense grief, not only within her family but throughout her nation.

Chapter 3

Escape from Guatemala

By the time she was twenty years old, Rigoberta Menchú had experienced a lifetime of horrors that would be impossible for most people in democratic nations to understand. She had worked twelve-hour days as a farm laborer when girls her age in the United States were entering third grade. When she was older, her father became a fugitive for his political beliefs, and her brother was tortured and burned to death in the town square. As an activist herself, Menchú lived a secret life, organizing Indians at the risk of death. Although she was naturally shy and humble, the young woman was not afraid to stand up at meetings and rallies and share the story of her struggles with others. And undeterred by the odds against her, Menchú educated herself, not only learning to read and write Spanish, but also spending countless hours debating topics such as religion, philosophy, capitalism, communism, democracy, and revolution with other activists.

In 1980 Menchú remained at the center of a deadly struggle between poor peasants and well-armed, highly trained professional soldiers. In this violent political struggle, Menchú, her siblings, and her parents were all targets. And they were not alone.

Menchú's eyes fill with tears as she recounts the murder of her family.

The torture, kidnapping, and killing of villagers in Quiché was escalating at a shocking rate, and hundreds of Maya were disappearing every month. Tired of watching helplessly, Vicente Menchú decided it would be better to die fighting than to live in fear. Although he had previously operated in secret, Vicente decided to attend a public demonstration that was organized in Guatemala City to protest the army's heavy presence in Quiché.

The Martyrdom of Vicente Menchú

On January 31, 1980, demonstrators took to the streets in the capital and engaged in several actions to draw widespread attention to their cause. Groups of revolutionaries with pistols and machetes seized several radio stations so they could announce their demands to the public. Another group entered the Spanish embassy and held several workers hostage. These actions were illegal, but as Stoll writes: "Taking hostages at embassies and government ministries is a common form of protest in Latin America. Even repressed or indifferent news media pay attention."[30]

The Spanish embassy was chosen as a target because the ambassador, Máximo Cajal y López, was sympathetic to the plight of the Indians. The takeover began at 11 A.M. when a group of masked protesters, including Vicente, walked into the embassy armed with machetes, several pistols, and Molotov cocktails, or firebombs.

Indigenous Life Irreparably Shredded

The Guatemalan civil war was in its twentieth year in 1980 when the government intensified its attacks against indigenous Maya in Quiché and other highland departments. This stepped-up program of violence resulted in the deaths of thousands of people, including Rigoberta Menchú's brother, mother, and father. In *Voices from Exile: Violence and Survival in Modern Maya History*, Victor Montejo describes the situation:

> The growing activity of the Guatemalan guerrilla groups . . . forced the Guatemalan military to rethink its strategy to preserve the status quo. Gen. Benedicto Lucas García, the president's brother, was responsible for drawing up plans for a massive campaign of strategic warfare against civilian populations thought to be collab-

orating with the guerrillas. . . . The army saw civilian populations, particularly Maya communities, as indistinguishable from guerrillas and guerrilla bases. The guerrilla group targeted was . . . the Guerrilla Army of the Poor, or EGP. . . . Under the new military plan, the worst excesses of military violence during the preceding decade became daily occurrences. Over the next eighteen months, four hundred highland villages would be eradicated, families torn apart, husbands tortured and murdered before their wives' eyes, women raped, babies bayoneted, fields, crops, and homes burned, and life in the highlands irreparably shredded.

Victor Montejo, *Voices from Exile: Violence and Survival in Modern Maya History*. Norman: University of Oklahoma Press, 1999, p. 43.

Despite the weapons, the takeover was nonviolent, and Cajal tried to negotiate a peaceful settlement to the dispute, speaking to Guatemalan president Lucas García by telephone. Authorities, however, cut the phone lines to the embassy as several hundred riot police surrounded the building. Around 2 P.M., police stormed the embassy, forcing twenty-eight protesters and ten hostages to retreat to a large meeting room on the second floor. At about 3 P.M., people in the streets heard a massive explosion and saw fire and smoke pouring out of the barred windows of the room.

The exact cause of the fire remains a matter of controversy. Government officials claim that one of the occupiers threw a

A woman bearing a cross with the name of a relative killed in the 1980 Spanish embassy massacre in Guatemala City weeps during a 2005 ceremony.

Molotov cocktail at the police as they tried to enter the room. Those who dispute this story say that the police fired an incendiary weapon, either a white phosphorus grenade or jellied gasoline called napalm. Whatever the case, fire and smoke quickly enveloped the victims, and police allowed no one to escape. When firefighters finally extinguished the flames, all but two of the thirty-eight men and women in the room were dead, including Vicente Menchú. Cajal, though badly burned, was one of the survivors. The other was a protester who was later kidnapped from the hospital and shot in the head.

Three days after the fire, a mass funeral was held in Guatemala City, and thousands of people attended. This outpouring of sympathy for the protesters from professionals, the poor, intellectuals, and the middle classes alike was unprecedented in Guatemalan history. When news footage of the conflagration was broadcast, it caused great harm to the government, as Stoll explains:

> [The] holocaust was not a defeat for the revolutionary movement. Because the police assaulted the building over the protests of the Spanish ambassador, the Guatemalan movement was held responsible for a violation of diplomatic immunity and the deaths of the people inside. Like no other event, the fire captured the brutality of the security forces and played it out in front of television cameras. The violation of international law was so flagrant that it made the Lucas García regime an intentional pariah. Within Guatemala, the massacre became a powerful symbol for pulling together a broad revolutionary coalition. The dead protesters were remembered as peasants struggling to protect their families from government kidnappers. They became exemplary victims, martyrs whose death presaged victory.[31]

The Death of Juana Tum

Grieving and fearful of official retaliation, Menchú and her family did not attend the public funeral in Guatemala City. And although she was devastated by her father's death, Menchú was not surprised and took consolation in the fact that he had not been tortured first.

In the aftermath of the fire, Vicente was honored as a martyr by millions of Guatemalan peasants. To carry on his work, a group of activist Catholics formed an organization known as the Vicente Menchú Revolutionary Christians. The group, which claimed four thousand members, combined religious beliefs with fierce revolutionary dogma, stating it would "exercise openly the just violence of the oppressed against those impeding the construction of the Kingdom of God."[32]

Rigoberta Menchú became a member of the Revolutionary Christians while continuing her work with the CUC. In February 1980 she helped organize a massive demonstration in southern Guatemala in which eighty thousand sugar and cotton workers went on strike against the fincas. The workers demanded a minimum wage of five quetzals a day. Although their demands were not met, after fifteen days the CUC received a signed agreement from powerful landlords stating they would raise the minimum wage to 3.20 quetzals.

This action did not go unnoticed by the government. With large groups of peasants successfully organizing, authorities began intensifying actions against indigenous communities, especially in Quiché and other departments in the highlands. Soldiers instituted a scorched-earth campaign that involved surrounding villages and firing high-powered weapons into Indians' houses. They also shot dogs, chickens, and other animals and used napalm to destroy crops growing in fields. To prevent retaliation from armed guerrillas, the military used Maya, many of them orphaned children, as human shields.

Chimel had not yet been destroyed, but villagers there were worried. In the twisted logic of the Guatemalan civil war, an entire village could be slated for destruction because of the actions of a few of its residents. And six of those who had occupied the Spanish embassy were from Chimel; another nine were from the surrounding region.

Despite the dangers, Menchú's mother, Juana Tum, was living in Chimel and attempting to continue her husband's work. On April 9, 1980, about six weeks after Vicente's death, Juana attended mass in the village church. Soon after, she was kidnapped by

Menchú's Revolutionary Christian Philosophy

The political organization called the Vicente Menchú Revolutionary Christians combined religious beliefs with militant political philosophies. Menchú explains what this melding of doctrines meant to her in *I, Rigoberta Menchú:*

> I'm one who walks on the Earth, not one who thinks that the Kingdom of God only comes after death. Through all my experiences, through everything I'd seen, through so much pain and suffering, I learned what the role of a Christian in the struggle is, and what the role of a Christian on this Earth is. We all came to important conclusions by studying the Bible. All our compañeros did. We discovered that the Bible has been used as a way of making us accept our situation, and not to bring enlightenment to the poor. The work of revolutionary Christians is above all to condemn and denounce the injustices committed against the people. . . . We also denounce the stance of the Church hierarchy because it is so often hand in glove with the government. . . . [They] call themselves Christians, yet they are often deaf to the suffering of the people. This is what I really meant . . . when I asked Christians to put into practice what being a Christian really means.

Rigoberta Menchú, *I, Rigoberta Menchú.* London: Verso, 1983, p. 245.

soldiers and repeatedly raped. Like her son, Juana was also methodically tortured and mutilated. After eight days of this brutal treatment, she was left under a tree, where she lay for several days before dying.

The January 31st Popular Front

In her autobiography Menchú describes the torture of her mother in vivid detail. However, although she was grief-stricken and bitter, she refused to give up fighting back: "For us," she wrote, "killing is something monstrous. And that's why we feel so angered by all the repression. Even more than that: our dedication to the struggle is a reaction against it, against all the suffering we endure."[33]

Menchú reacted to her mother's death by renewing her efforts against the government. In mid-1980 she joined a newly formed group that united guerrillas, student groups, and Indian organizations. In honor of Vicente and the others who had died in the embassy fire, the organization was named the January 31st Popular Front (FP-31). Menchú describes the objectives of the group:

> We wanted to weaken the government economically, politically, and militarily. We weakened them economically by our actions in that, although the workers carry on working, they tamper with their machines or break parts. Small things that drain economic resources. . . . We boycott anything we can, or destroy

Menchú, having lost both her parents and a brother to government forces, became a hunted woman and had to flee the country.

a coffee estate, or a cotton estate, depending on the attitude of the landowner. . . . Our actions weaken the regime military too. We try to split up the armed forces so that not only do they have to attack our politico-military organizations, but they have to spread themselves to attack us as well.[34]

The first attempt by the FP-31 to undermine the government occurred on the first of May, a day that is traditionally used to celebrate working people. The plan was to create chaos throughout the capital and bring commerce to a halt without injuring or killing anyone. As part of an FP-31 action team, Menchú was assigned to set up a barricade on a busy road and snarl traffic. With motorists trapped in their cars, activists set off what Menchú calls "propaganda bombs." This involved showering the captive motorists with hundreds of leaflets and holding short political rallies called lightning meetings. Each propaganda bomb action lasted only a few minutes since activists had to leave before police arrived ready to shoot them. Through the use of detailed planning, the FP-31 proved successful in keeping police forces moving from place to place without ever apprehending any protesters.

On the second of May another part of the plan went into effect when activists phoned in bomb threats to hundreds of factories throughout the nation. Although no actual bombs were placed in factories, the resulting panic virtually shut down Guatemala's economy for five days as the bomb threats continued.

A Hunted Woman

Despite the temporary success of the FP-31 demonstrations, the revolution was going badly in Guatemala. Leaders were disappearing and meeting horrific deaths at the hands of government interrogators. Of the thirty people who founded the CUC in 1978, only six were still alive in 1981. Those who survived quit politics, went into hiding, or left the country. And while thousands of Maya secretly supported antigovernment actions, most were afraid to speak up or join the demonstrations.

Because of her work, Menchú was a hunted woman, and most people were afraid to associate with her for fear of being arrested and tortured. In the capital, however, she found a few people who were willing to house her for a day or two at a time. During this extremely stressful period Menchú developed a peptic ulcer, a condition that causes chronic symptoms such as vomiting, nausea, heartburn, and abdominal pain.

In early 1981, when she had tired of hiding in the city, Menchú decided she would blend in better in the town of Huehuetenango, which had a Maya majority. However, after she arrived there, a group of soldiers spotted her as she walked down the street. They pursued her, but she managed to elude them by ducking into a church. After hiding for several hours, Menchú made her way back to Guatemala City. There, using a false identity, she took work as a maid in a convent.

Alone, physically ill, and grief-stricken over the loss of her family, Menchú was plagued by nightmares, guilt, and thoughts of suicide. As she writes in her second book, *Crossing Borders*, "I didn't want to know anything about anything. Not about faith, or life, or prayer. . . . I felt totally empty. I saw the future as an immense darkness. . . . When you lose your home you lose a piece of your life."[35]

After several weeks in the convent, Menchú regained her strength by reminding herself of the sacrifices made by her father and her *compañeros*. By that time government spies were making regular visits to the convent, and Menchú felt that for the nuns' safety, she had to leave.

Using her network of covert political contacts, Menchú was able to raise enough money to buy an airplane ticket to Mexico City. Since she could not travel under her own name, dressed in traditional Mayan clothing, Menchú assumed the identity of a ladino woman. She bought stylish new clothes, cut her long hair and had it processed with a curly permanent, and obtained a counterfeit passport.

Menchú had never seen an airplane up close and was amazed when she was able to board without harassment by authorities. Once in the air, Menchú cried with relief. The hunted woman was leaving a life of desperation far behind her.

Recovery and Reunion

Menchú was accompanied on her journey by a nun, Sister Gládis. When they landed in Mexico City, the sister introduced

Menchú to several bishops, including Samuel Ruiz and Méndez Arceo. The two took the women to a conference of Catholic bishops in mid-1981. Although Menchú was very timid and did not speak Spanish well, she gave several speeches in which she described the deaths of her parents and brother and expressed her desperation, pain, and anguish.

Menchú's talks were so moving that bishops from Venezuela, Brazil, and Ecuador asked her to tell her story in those nations. Moreover, Ruiz, the bishop of Chiapas, a Mexican state bordering Guatemala, invited Menchú to live as a member of his household. Moving to Chiapas was a logical choice for Menchú, since she wanted to remain among her own people. The state had been part of Guatemala until 1824 and the region was populated by hundreds of thousands of Maya, many of whom were Guatemalan exiles seeking asylum in Mexico. She gladly accepted Ruiz's offer.

Mayan refugees gather at the cathedral in San Cristóbal de las Casas, Mexico, where Menchú was offered asylum.

Ruiz lived in the town of San Cristóbal de las Casas, and once there Menchú was befriended by the bishop's sister, Doña Lucha, who treated her as a daughter. For the first time in years, Menchú felt safe and secure, but she continued to suffer as a result of traumatic experiences she had endured. Small noises sounded to her like bullets being fired, and she was unable to sleep without having nightmares. Eventually, a doctor gave her sleeping pills, and Menchú slept for days while Lucha and Ruiz cared for her. During her waking hours, the young Guatemalan told Lucha about all that she had been through.

After several weeks, Menchú felt better and began traveling from village to village with Ruiz as he did his pastoral work. This not only helped her regain a positive outlook on life but also gave her a broader perspective concerning her heritage. Growing up in Guatemala, Menchú had lived among Maya who identified themselves mainly by their individual tribes. In Mexico, however, Menchú came to realize that her tribe was part of a larger culture of Maya that spanned national borders and possessed its own proud collective history and identity.

Exile

[Rigoberta] never went to school as a child; neither did I. When she was 8, she migrated to coastal plantations to pick coffee and cotton; so did I. Like her I did not learn Spanish until I was in my late teens. She is an exile; so am I.

Quoted in Zygmunt Baumann, *Memories of Class.* London: Routledge & Kegan Paul, 1982, p. 1.

Menchú also embraced part of her own family's heritage. Her mother, Juana, had been a midwife, healer, and herbal doctor in Chimel. In Chiapas, Menchú took nursing courses taught by nuns and worked for a time with a group of traveling health workers.

Menchú's new way of life was exciting, but nothing brought her more joy than the discovery that her two little sisters, Anita, ten, and Lucía, thirteen, were alive in Guatemala. With the help of Ruiz, Menchú was soon reunited with them in Chiapas for the Christmas 1980 holiday. During their reunion Menchú learned that after the death of their mother, the young girls, like so many other orphans,

Menchú dons traditional native garb before a public appearance.

were adopted by the Guerrilla Army of the Poor. As a result, although they were very young, the sisters were politically aware and militant in their revolutionary beliefs.

Back to Guatemala

Anita and Lucía continued to participate in politics in their new surroundings. On a two-week trip to Mexico City, Menchú and her sisters were filmed for the first time. Using assumed names, they were interviewed for Mexican television about their experiences. The Menchús also spoke on the radio and were honored at a dinner hosted by Alaïda Foppa, a Guatemalan writer and intellectual who disappeared only two days later upon returning home.

Despite the attention, Menchú was having a difficult time caring for her sisters. They bickered, and both were unhappy in Mexico. They continually talked about their parents and begged Menchú to take them back to Guatemala. Performing political work with Ruiz among the Guatemalan refugees in Chiapas had restored Menchú's interest in political action. She decided that the time was right to return home, though the three sisters had less than ten dollars among them.

Seeking Answers

We took religion very seriously . . . so when her family members died, she took it to the chapel. There were moments of rebellion when she shouted: "Why is it that my family has to disappear!"

Quoted in David Stoll, *Rigoberta Menchú and the Story of All Poor Guatemalans.* Boulder, CO: Westview Press, 1998, p. 164.

Upon returning to Guatemala City through a clandestine guerrilla network, the Menchús immediately went to work with the Vicente Menchú Revolutionary Christians. The organization had adopted a new slogan meant to convey the groups' intentions to the world: "Clear Head, Caring Heart, Fighting Fist of Rural Workers." Menchú explains the meaning the first two terms had for her:

> "Clear Head" not only showed respect for knowledge in general, it also meant we had to study the underlying causes of problems. With a clear head, I learned to take the initiative, propose solutions, think my ideas through and justify my thinking. . . . ["Caring Heart"] meant showing compassion for others, being tolerant, making our own lives an example of humanity.[36]

Despite her revitalized commitment to the revolution, Menchú was unable to stay in Guatemala for long because she committed a serious error. While the three sisters were moving the belongings of the Revolutionary Christians from one safe house to another in a rented van, they forgot to tie down a box filled with political leaflets. When the flyers scattered across the highway, Menchú was sure that the papers would either quickly be discovered by police or that the driver of the van, who worked for the rental company, would turn her and her sisters in for a reward. Although neither scenario came to pass, members of the Revolutionary Christians, angry over the blunder and afraid that protecting the Menchús was too much of a risk, refused to shelter them any longer. Anita and Lucía returned to Quiché to rejoin the guerrilla army. Rigoberta traveled overland through Honduras to Nicaragua, where she registered with the United Nations High Commission as a refugee and was provided with a UN passport.

A Highly Valued Perspective

In 1982, after a short stay in Nicaragua, Menchú began a nomadic existence that lasted for twelve years. Traveling with all of her possessions packed into a single suitcase, she visited many countries in Latin America, where she gave speeches about the plight of Maya in Guatemala. Menchú's first stop was Mexico City, where she joined the international committee of the CUC and also began working with two other groups, the Christian Coordinating Committee for Solidarity with Guatemala and the Guatemala Committee for Patriotic Unity. These organizations allowed Menchú to closely follow the refugee situation at home, which was growing worse every day. Tens of thousands of homeless people, mostly widows, orphans, and the elderly, were being harassed by the army. With nowhere to stay, they were dying from malnutrition, malaria, and infections. Some of these refugees were from Chimel, which by this time had been razed by the military.

In Mexico, Menchú's colleagues were ministers, poets, writers, political leaders, and professors. Through her discussions with them, Menchú developed a deep understanding of Guatemalan history, democracy, and multiculturalism, as well as international law. Because Menchú had first-hand knowledge of Guatemalan repression, her perspective was highly valued by the professionals. She was often called upon to give speeches and share her viewpoint

Guatemalan children endure their rootless existence in a refugee camp. Menchú, a refugee herself, shared her story with the world.

during meetings. While this was largely a positive experience, it was also a sad one. Like many of the people she worked with, Menchú had lost family members and dozens of friends in sense-less violence.

Menchú could easily have been counted among Guatemala's anonymous dead. As fate would have it, however, she was a sur-vivor, and one who was uniquely qualified to help end the civil war in her homeland. By escaping the death squads and leaving Guatemala, Menchú had taken the first steps on the long road of recovery and renewal. In the years that followed, the young orphaned refugee would share her personal story with millions, crossing borders to shine a bright light on the dark history of Guatemalan politics.

Chapter 4

Telling Her Story to the World

Between 1982 and 1983 Rigoberta Menchú's life changed dramatically as she left behind the life of a poor Guatemalan exile and took on the role of international champion of indigenous rights. The transformation began in Mexico City, where Menchú met activists from the Netherlands, France, and elsewhere who were organizing Guatemalan independence groups in Europe. These political workers arranged for Menchú to accompany them on a ten-nation speaking tour of Europe, where she acted as the representative of the January 31st Popular Front.

When Menchú embarked on this tour, she was not well known among activists and was unaccustomed to being treated as an equal by white people. As she writes in *Crossing Borders*, "When you're born in a racist country, you have no sense of your own worth. You're afraid of everything and think everybody is superior."[37] However, Latin American historian Arturo Taracena, whom she met in Paris, believed Menchú's compelling story was one that the world needed to hear. Taracena encouraged Menchú to write a book about her experiences, but since she did not have the literacy skills to do so, he introduced her to Venezuelan-born anthropologist Elisabeth Burgos, who

Menchú smiles often but her smile quickly fades when she talks of her ordeals.

would act as an interviewer and editor. The resulting book, *I, Rigoberta Menchú: An Indian Woman in Guatemala* brought Menchú undreamed-of recognition.

Talking About Dramatic Events

Although Burgos was from a wealthy family, she shared common experiences with Menchú. Burgos had also been harassed by a right-wing military government for her political beliefs and had seen many friends killed by government forces. Unlike Menchú, however, Burgos was a sophisticated activist who had worked for the international Communist Party throughout Latin America. In the 1960s she supported leftist guerrillas in Venezuela and trained with Argentinean revolutionary Che Guevara with the goal of fomenting revolution in the Third World. Burgos also spent a great deal of time in Cuba working with Cuban dictator Fidel Castro, who sponsored military training for Guatemalan guerrillas. It was in Cuba that Burgos befriended Guatemalan revolutionaries and learned about the indigenous cause.

Trials and Traditions

In the classroom, Menchú's work has made vivid both the Mayan traditions and the more recent trials of Mayan peoples in the face of genocidal military incursions.

Quoted in Robert Strauss, "Truth and Consequences," May/June 1999, *Stanford Magazine*, www.stanfordalumni.org/news/magazine/1999/mayjune/articles/Menchú.html.

By the time Menchú met Burgos, her life as a revolutionary was in the past and she was a middle-class professional whose husband was a foreign policy adviser to the president of France. Nonetheless, Burgos was a strong supporter of indigenous rights and worked to organize political fund-raisers for Guatemalan activists in Paris.

Menchú first arrived at Burgos's Paris apartment in January 1982. Although it was cold and snowing, Menchú wore only a light cape and her traditional Mayan outfit, which was suitable for a tropical climate. Beyond her attire, Menchú gave a mixed impression, as Burgos writes:

> The first thing that struck me about her was her open, almost childlike smile. Her face was round and moon-shaped. Her expression was as guileless as that of a child and a smile hovered permanently on her lips. She looked

astonishingly young. I later discovered that her youthful air soon faded when she had to talk about the dramatic events that had overtaken her family. When she talked about that, you could see the suffering in her eyes, they lost their youthful sparkle and became the eyes of a mature woman who has known what it means to suffer.[38]

For seven days, the young Guatemalan woman told the story of her life to Burgos, who recorded the words on cassette tapes. Menchú spoke of her political activism during the civil war and the tragic deaths of her brother, mother, and father. She also told Burgos about the traditions of her people, their beliefs concerning the supernatural, and Mayan attitudes toward life, love, birth, and death. Concerning the selection of the topics, Burgos writes: "She talked to me not only because she wanted to tell us about her suf-

Meeting Rigoberta Menchú

Elisabeth Burgos edited the book *I, Rigoberta Menchú: An Indian Woman in Guatemala*. In the introduction, Burgos describes her first meeting with the author:

She came to my home one evening in January 1982. She was wearing traditional costume, including a multicolored *huipil* [blouse] with rich and varied embroidery. . . . She was also wearing an ankle-length skirt; this too was multicolored and the thick material was obviously hand-woven. I later learned that it was called a *corte*. She had a broad, brightly-colored sash around her waist. On her head, she wore a fuschia and red scarf knotted behind her neck. When she left Paris, she gave it to me, telling me that it had taken her three months to weave the cloth. Around her neck she had an enormous necklace of red beads and old silver coins with a heavy solid silver cross dangling from it. I remember it as being a particularly cold night; in fact I think it was snowing. Rigoberta was wearing no stockings and no coat. Beneath her *huipil*, her arms were bare. Her only protection against the cold was a short cape made from imitation traditional fabric; it barely came to her waist.

Rigoberta Menchú, *I, Rigoberta Menchú*, ed. Elisabeth Burgos, trans. Ann Wright. London: Verso, 1984, p. xiv.

ferings but also—or perhaps mainly—because she wanted us to hear about her culture."[39]

Menchú spoke freely, with little prompting from Burgos, and when her story was finished, it filled more than eighteen hours of tape. After the sessions were over, Burgos typed out every word on the cassette tapes exactly as they were spoken. The final text in Spanish filled nearly five hundred pages. By reading through the manuscript several times, Burgos was able to identify major themes, such as family, cultural traditions, education, work, political events, and so on. Burgos deleted her interview questions, organized the material into chapters, and was left with a monologue—Menchu's narrative of her life story.

After the initial manuscript of *I, Rigoberta Menchú: An Indian Woman in Guatemala* was completed, Menchú says she spent about two months editing it. She writes in *Crossing Borders:* "It was painful to have to relive the content of the book. I censored several parts that might have been dangerous for people. I took out bits that referred to my village, details about my brothers and sisters, and names of people. . . . Giving their names away in a book could have had them killed."[40]

After the text was revised, *I, Rigoberta Menchú* was published in Spanish in 1983 and in French and English the next year. By 2000 at least 250,000 copies of the French and English versions had been sold, with many additional copies printed in German, Italian, Dutch, Japanese, Swedish, Russian, and Arabic. But much to Menchú's dismay, Burgos retained the full author's copyright to the story and was paid 50 percent of the royalties. This resulted in a break in the friendship between Menchú and Burgos that has never been repaired.

When the Mountains Tremble

About the time *I, Rigoberta Menchú* was published, Menchú was asked to participate in *When the Mountains Tremble*, a documentary film about the civil war in Guatemala. Filmed by Pamela Yates and Newton Thomas Sigel in the early 1980s, the movie shows the stark reality of life for peasants in the war-torn country. The film also explores the role the United States played in the war by providing money, arms, and training to the

Guatemalan government. Some of the atrocities depicted in the movie are described by reviewer Eric DC:

> Indian [peasants] explain how their village was . . . pillaged before being burnt to the ground. They now try to survive in the mountains, keeping lookouts for any signs of an impeding army. The filmmakers acquired eerie black & white footage of government henchmen carrying out disappearances and police in gas masks gassing protestors while beating them with batons. The climax of the film begins with a series of grim pictures drawn by Indian children showing the horrors they have personally witnessed. This then leads into a [heart wrenching scene] of a village that has had its "subversives"executed by a local army unit. Despite this horror the image that leaves the most lasting impression is that of a mother with a baby slung on her back foraging through a trash dump as incoming trucks unload practically on top of her.[41]

A scene from the documentary When the Mountains Tremble *shows mourners at a funeral for Guatemalan victims of government oppression.*

Mayan girls in native dress appear in the documentary on Guatemala's civil war. Menchú's own testimony in the film is compelling.

The searing footage in *When the Mountains Tremble* provided a powerful visual record of the events described in *I, Rigoberta Menchú*. Menchú, however, was not an original member of the project. She was asked to participate only after Yates and Sigel had read her book after the film was nearly finished. To incorporate her testimony into the movie, the filmmakers shot footage of Menchú talking about the deaths of her family members, peasant hardships, and the politics of rich and poor in Guatemala. Sitting in front of a stark black backdrop and dressed in her colorful traditional clothing, Menchú is compelling and credible on screen, trembling with anger and grief as she recalls the horrors in her past.

When the film was released in 1984 it shocked audiences in the United States and Europe, where people were largely unaware of the situation in Guatemala. The film won a Special Jury Prize for Documentaries at the 1984 Sundance Film Festival in Park City,

Utah. It also won the Special Jury Award at the USA Film Festival in Dallas.

Indigenous Rights and Traditional Cultures

After her brief role in film, the International Indian Treaty Council, an organization founded by Native Americans, invited Menchú to the United States. According to the council's Web site, the San Francisco–based group "is an organization of Indigenous Peoples from North, Central, South America and the Pacific working for the Sovereignty and Self-Determination of Indigenous Peoples and the recognition and protection of Indigenous Rights, Traditional Cultures and Sacred Lands."[42] Menchú was warmly welcomed by members of the treaty council when she arrived at their annual meeting to represent two organizations, the international CUC and the United Representation of the Guatemalan Opposition (RUOG), a group started by exiles. As a guest of the council, Menchú participated in American Indian rituals such as purification in a sweat lodge and smoking a sacred pipe. When she spoke at a meeting about her experiences in Guatemala, many council members openly wept.

Members of the treaty council asked Menchú to accompany them to Geneva, Switzerland, where they were scheduled to attend a United Nations conference concerning indigenous rights. The group in charge of the conference was called the United Nations Working Group on Indigenous Peoples, and, as Menchú writes, they had very little clout with the ambassadors and other UN workers:

> There were very few indigenous people at the UN in those days. We looked like oddballs and we were treated as such. Some officials were offhand and rather suspicious, as if we were making things up. I think they were embarrassed for us. Others were curious to find out what we had come to the UN for. Non-indigenous friends fighting for indigenous rights were

few and far between in those days. For many people, we were insignificant.[43]

"A Cold, Cold Place"

Despite the lowly status of native peoples among the UN bureaucrats, Menchú was instrumental in establishing the first indigenous Guatemalan presence at the UN. However, when a Norwegian diplomat requested that she give a speech to UN delegates, it was interrupted by the Guatemalan ambassador, who

A young Mayan refugee carries his sister on his back. Menchú brought the plight of such refugees onto the world stage.

In 1986 Vinicio Cerezo became the first civilian president elected in Guatemala after thirty-two years of military rule.

used bureaucratic wrangling to halt it. Eventually, however, Menchú was allowed to make her presentation.

With ladino bureaucrats opposing her presence at the UN, Menchú started disassociating herself from the Guatemalan guerrilla movement. Instead, she took on the role of a human rights advocate for indigenous peoples. As such, she began to draw international attention to the plight of the Maya in Guatemala. Using her new status as a member of Working Group on Indigenous Peoples and the RUOG, Menchú spoke to politicians, foreign ministers, and international human rights organizations. Her goal was to see democratic nations condemn Guatemala's dictatorship and impose economic and bureaucratic sanctions against it.

The job was never easy. Negotiating the dense maze of UN bureaucracy to talk to officials who were often either indifferent or hostile frequently left Menchú feeling hopeless, depressed, and weary. Her despair was compounded when she learned that the Guatemalans were competing for official attention with many other persecuted groups from El Salvador, Colombia, East Timor, Afghanistan, and the Middle East. These groups had also suffered rape, torture, murder, and eviction from their ancestral homelands. Commenting on the situation, Menchú writes: "Lives became a game of statistics. . . . It was a cold, cold place, as if the cold of the snow had penetrated the bodies of the diplomats when it came to the subject of human rights. If four hundred burned Guatemalan villages didn't move them, what would?"[44]

Arrested in Guatemala

Apathetic official attitudes aside, things did improve slightly for the Guatemalans. According to Stoll: "Via the innumerable conferences worked by Rigoberta and her confederates, international pressure eventually obliged the Guatemalan army to negotiate with guerrillas and accept UN observers throughout the country."[45]

In 1986 those observers oversaw the election of Vinicio Cerezo as the first civilian president of Guatemala after thirty-two years of military rule. The popular former mayor of Guatemala City, Cerezo received 70 percent of the vote. However, generals continued to dominate the government, and many observers felt that Cerezo simply provided cover for the military so that Guatemala could gain acceptance by the international community. As Menchú wrote in April 1987: "The civilian government is giving the military more time, legitimacy, money, and a political space internationally which in the past it had no chance of obtaining because of its bad reputation and isolation."[46]

A year after Menchú wrote those words, she returned to Guatemala with several American and European politicians and members of the RUOG. Although she feared she would be arrested and killed, Menchú had been asked to return home by the Guatemalan ambassador to the United Nations, who was hoping to advertise the positive changes made by the civilian government. This show of goodwill never materialized—Menchú was met at the airport by four hundred heavily armed police officers, who arrested her on the orders of Cerezo.

Menchú was put into a car with blacked out windows and taken to the judicial courts building in the capital. There she was questioned by the judge who had ordered her father's arrest in 1970 and who was responsible for ordering the executions of thousands of Guatemalan peasants. Menchú refused to talk to the judge without a defense attorney, but after contacting a lawyer's association, the archbishop, and the Guatemalan procurator for human rights, she could find no one brave enough to represent her. After several hours, however, Menchú finally found a lawyer, Harold Vitelio Fuentes, to defend her.

Truth and Drama

[Rigoberta's] narrative strategy is easy to defend because her most important claims, about the Guatemalan army's killings, are true. Rigoberta was dramatizing her life . . . in order to have an impact.

David Stoll, *Rigoberta Menchú and the Story of All Poor Guatemalans*. Boulder, CO: Westview Press, 1998, p. 273.

Menchú faced three serious charges. One was for public disorder, related to organizing peasants to rebel against the government and putting national security at risk in the municipalities of Nebaj, Cotzal, and Uspantán. Menchú felt this charge was ridiculous since she had not been in those areas in more than eight years. The second charge was that she wrote papers that contained Marxist ideas, which was against the law in Guatemala.

The third charge stated that Menchú had collaborated with antigovernment guerrillas and that she had been a commander and military instructor at guerrilla training camps in Nicaragua and Cuba. This was the most serious charge—others who had been convicted of this crime had been tortured and killed. Unlike those people, however, Menchú was now famous. Few believed the contrived charges against her, and three thousand people gathered outside the judicial courts building in protest.

The European politicians who had accompanied Menchú acted to help her. One of them called François Mitterrand, the president of France, who personally intervened on Menchú's behalf. Other politicians from Europe and the United States also phoned Cerezo. After eight hours in police custody, Menchú was released.

A Nomination for a Respected Prize

Menchú stayed in Guatemala for one week but lived in fear the entire time. Yet, her release from jail had shown her that her fame could protect her from open government retribution as she worked to focus international attention on the dismal situation in her homeland. Instead of avoiding Guatemala and working from the safety of her home in Mexico City, Menchú continued to return to her native country several times a year. In February 1989 she was a delegate for the RUOG at a national dialogue sponsored by the church. During this stay Menchú received death threats from anonymous sources, including a bouquet with an invitation to her own funeral. She managed to leave the country for Italy less than an hour before a car bomb exploded outside the house where she had stayed.

Once Menchú arrived in Italy she was offered a diplomatic seat in the Italian parliament. This granted her some safety when traveling because she was issued a diplomatic passport, which protects the bearer from arrest while performing diplomatic duties. In a further act of respect, a group of Italians signed a petition nominating Menchú for the Nobel Peace Prize. This nomination was supported by Amnesty International as well as several groups in Italy that advocated Guatemalan indigenous rights. When told of the nomination, Menchú says she laughed and said: "Only important people win the Nobel Prize."[47]

The momentum to award Menchú a Peace Prize grew over the next several years. However, her chances of winning appeared slim because more than one hundred of the most respected leaders in the world are nominated for the prize every year. So although she was honored by the nomination, Menchú disregarded it as she continued to work for indigenous rights.

Five Hundred Years of Resistance

Menchú's next big project concerned plans throughout Latin America to honor Christopher Columbus on the five hundredth anniversary, or quincentenary, of his first voyage to the Americas in 1492. In Guatemala, quincentenary festivities were being planned by a government panel called the Spanish Commission.

On the 500-year anniversary of Christopher Columbus's arrival in the Americas, Menchú (center left) leads a march against the oppression of indigenous peoples.

Since the celebration ignored the harm Spanish colonization had done to indigenous people, Menchú and her colleagues were strongly opposed to it, as she explains in *Crossing Borders:*

> Our people said that there wasn't anything to cele-brate. On the contrary, the occasion offended us and generations of our ancestors. It was no cause for cele-bration, and even less a meeting of two cultures. We wanted to commemorate our ancestors, and remem-ber them with a dignity worthy of the coming centu-ry. If the Spanish Commission thought the date was so

Five Hundred Years of Resistance

During the Five Hundred Years of Resistance meetings held between 1989 and 1992, Rigoberta Menchú found that indigenous people held a common vision and shared demands. She describes her feelings about this community in *Crossing Borders:*

> Our community is the reason why we are still alive, why we are still here five hundred years after the Conquest. We have survived amid the rubble of endless massacres. If our peoples had disintegrated, if they had lost their languages, if they had lost their communities, their collective way of life, their concept of leadership, they would have died out. We discovered that if we unite . . . we will achieve the results we seek.
>
> We also discovered that we have not simply been spectators during these five hundred years. We have been protagonists as well. We realized how often our intellectual rights have been usurped, how our thinking has been manipulated and distorted. Since 1989, the world has rediscovered indigenous wisdom. This is a source of pride for us. I am pleased that the thoughts and lives of our peoples have become more widely known.

Rigoberta Menchú, *Crossing Borders.* New York: Verso, 1998, p. 170.

Menchú celebrates Latin America's indigenous populations.

important, they should have given us the opportunity
to participate as protagonists in our own history.[48]

To counter the anniversary celebration, Menchú organized a
1989 conference of indigenous people from Ecuador, Colombia,
Brazil, and Guatemala. Together these groups founded the Five
Hundred Years of Resistance campaign to celebrate the heritage
and accomplishments of indigenous people as well as their battles
against colonialism. In 1991 another Five Hundred Years conference was held in Quetzaltenango, Guatemala, attracting twenty-
five thousand people from throughout Latin America. Since many
new members were people of African descent from the Caribbean
and elsewhere, the name of the organization was updated to Five
Hundred Years of Indigenous, Black and Popular Resistance.

During this meeting in Guatemala's second-largest city, members of youth groups, feminist organizations, human rights groups,
solidarity committees, and church councils held a huge parade to
demonstrate their unity. When Menchú appeared, people cheered
and screamed her name, treating her as a conquering hero. There
was talk that she might run for president, and hundreds of foreign
reporters lined up to interview her.

After ten years of working selflessly, tirelessly, and anonymous-
ly for indigenous rights, Menchú had achieved a unique status as
a Mayan leader. Unlike the privileged officials at the UN or the
bureaucrats within the Guatemalan government, Menchú had
climbed to the top from the lowest rung in society. And it was the
memory of those who had died in the struggle that gave her the
strength to face her fears and fight for the rights of her people.

Chapter 5

The Nobel Laureate

By the early 1990s Rigoberta Menchú's ten-year campaign for indigenous rights in Guatemala had made her a well-known figure. Her travels had taken her to the United States, Central and South America, and Europe, and wherever she traveled she was treated as a celebrity. Menchú's life story and her human rights work received so much attention that she was nominated for the Nobel Peace Prize for the first time in 1989. In 1991 two Nobel laureates, Argentinean human rights advocate Adolfo Pérez Esquivel and South African antiapartheid activist Desmond Tutu, again nominated Menchú. Joining these respected laureates were the entire Norwegian parliament and a group of activists and scholars from both Italy and England. In addition, Menchú had the backing of religious leaders from both the Catholic and Evangelical churches.

Like other events in Menchú's life, the Nobel nomination was not without controversy. Those who opposed her nomination wondered how a peace prize could be given to someone who belonged to an organization that threw Molotov cocktails, made bomb threats, and menaced the lives of suspected informants. Menchú was also closely aligned with guerrillas who kidnapped and killed landowners and public officials.

"A Badge of Legitimacy"

Menchú's Nobel nomination was even controversial among her colleagues, sparking a debate concerning the prize at the 1991 Five Hundred Years of Resistance conference in Guatemala. Menchú writes that when a resolution was put forth to support her Nobel candidacy: "Many . . . brothers and sisters did not agree with my candidacy. They said, 'Who does she represent? Who made her a leader? Who elected her?'"[49] Ironically, Menchú was suffering from laryngitis during the long, contentious debate about the measure and could not speak to defend herself. In the end, however, the resolution was passed.

The support pleased Menchú because she felt that even if she did not win the prize, the attention would provide her with an international platform from which to denounce human rights abuses in Guatemala. And, as Stoll writes, it allowed her to travel freely in her native land:

> Inside Guatemala, the nomination could be used as a badge of legitimacy to organize an intimidated population. It was a sign of international recognition that might encourage ordinary Guatemalans to express themselves, like a wedge cracking open a wall of silence. . . . Flanked by the foreign escorts in her entourage, Rigoberta stepped up her visits, and the popular organizations turned out crowds to greet her. Doubtless there were army officers who wanted to put a stop to the spectacle, but the high command was not so rash as to blow up a Nobel candidate.[50]

During this time, the Guatemalan government accelerated its negotiations with several guerrilla organizations in hopes of ending the civil war. While this may not have been a result of Menchú's growing fame, the talks took place at a time when international attention was focused on Guatemala because of Menchú's Nobel candidacy.

Menchú gives a lecture in Spain in 2005. Nobel recognition of the activist made her a world-renowned figure.

"We Love You Mayan Daughter"

In June 1992 an international committee with hundreds of members was formed to promote Menchú's Nobel nomination, and by early October the speculation about the Nobel Prize had grown to a fevered pitch in Guatemala. When Menchú arrived in Guatemala City on October 9, thousands turned out to greet her at the airport. During this visit Menchú was consumed with her usual human rights activism, this time working with a group called the National Coordinating Committee of Guatemalan Widows, composed of women whose husbands had been killed in political violence. Many of the group's activities required Menchú to speak at meetings in the interior of the country, where the civil war continued unabated. In the past, when Menchú had traveled into these areas she was at risk not only from government forces but also from guerrillas who might kidnap her to satisfy their own political agendas. However, on this journey, everywhere she went people lined the roadways to

Showing solidarity with other Guatemalans, Menchú marches during a demonstration.

watch her motorcade pass, and thousands turned out for demonstrations wherever she spoke. Many held signs that read "We love you, Rigoberta, with or without the prize," and shouted "We love you Mayan daughter, with or without."[51] Churches rang their bells, and bystanders set off fireworks.

A Vivid Symbol of Peace

On October 14 Menchú was in the town of San Marcos when the Norwegian ambassador to Mexico called to notify her that she had been awarded the Peace Prize. She was the first indigenous person to receive this distinction and, at the age of thirty-three, the youngest recipient ever. The official committee statement lauded Menchú's achievements and said that she "stands out as a vivid symbol of peace and reconciliation across ethnic, cultural and social dividing lines, in her own country, on the American continent and in the world."[52]

The next day, more than fifteen thousand people assembled to hear Menchú speak in Guatemala City. Although Menchú invited President Jorge Serrano Elías to attend, he chose to ignore the rally and made no comment concerning the rowdy celebrations that were taking place throughout the country. However, an army spokesman accused Menchú of "supporting or belonging to the country's rebel leftist movement," and foreign minister Gonzalo Menendez made a statement saying Menchú should have been disqualified for the Peace Prize because "she is tied to certain groups that have endangered Guatemala."[53] In some regions the army even organized rallies to protest Menchú's winning of the award. She countered the criticisms by saying that while she supported the insurrection, she never fought with the guerrillas.

The Nobel Peace Prize

The Norwegian Nobel Committee has decided to award the Nobel Peace Prize for 1992 to Rigoberta Menchú from Guatemala in recognition of her work for social justice and ethno-cultural reconciliation based on respect for the rights of indigenous peoples.

Quoted in Tim Golden, "Guatemala Indian Wins the Nobel Peace Prize," *New York Times*, October 17, 1992, p. 1.

Although her award was greeted with little enthusiasm by her own government, Menchú received wide praise from other leaders, including the presidents of France and Italy; Boutros Boutros-Ghali, secretary-general of the United Nations; and Pope John Paul II. For several days at least, Guatemala was at peace as the foreign press and international dignitaries acknowledged the long struggle that Menchú represented.

The Rigoberta Menchú Tum Foundation

Menchú used the monetary award from the Peace Prize to establish the Rigoberta Menchú Tum Foundation. In doing so, the Nobel laureate said that she wanted to honor the memory of her father, campaign for peace, and revive indigenous culture in Guatemala. The foundation had an ambitious agenda that included full participation in the ongoing peace negotiations and the integration of war-scarred citizens back into Guatemalan society. Menchú also

Rigoberta Menchú's Nobel Prize Acceptance Speech

In December 1992, Rigoberta Menchú gave a speech to the Nobel Committee in which she conveyed what winning the Nobel Peace Prize meant to her. The speech is excerpted below from the Nobelprize.org Web site:

In addition to being a priceless treasure, [the Nobel Peace Prize] is an instrument with which to fight for peace, for justice, for the rights of those who suffer the abysmal economical, social, cultural and political inequalities, typical of the order of the world in which we live. . . .

This Nobel Prize represents a standard bearer that encourages us to continue denouncing the violation of Human Rights, committed against the people in Guatemala, in America and in the world, and to perform a positive role in respect of the pressing task in my country, which is to achieve peace with social justice. . . .

There is no doubt whatsoever that it constitutes a sign of hope in the struggle of the indigenous people in the entire Continent.
It is also a tribute to the Central-American people who are still searching for their stability, for the structuring of their future, and the path for their development and integration, based on civil democracy and mutual respect.

Quoted in Nobelprize.org, "Rigoberta Menchú Tum: The Nobel Peace Prize 1992: Nobel Lecture," 1992. http://nobelprize.org/nobel_prizes/peace/laureates/1992/tum-lecture.html.

Menchú proudly displays her 1992 Nobel Peace Prize diploma and gold medal after receiving them from Nobel Committee chairman Francis Sejersted.

planned to use the foundation to support indigenous civil liberties, including the rights to land, cultural autonomy, education, health care, and greater access to the national courts. Moreover, according to the group's Web site, the foundation promised to be the first Guatemalan organization to promote indigenous women's rights, including "equality in all areas, health care, education, culture, identity, [the] right to own land and the right to organize."[54]

The foundation was immediately put to the test in January 1993, when large groups of Guatemalan exiles began returning home from Mexico. The repatriation was part of an agreement signed between representatives of the exiles and the Guatemalan government. The Rigoberta Menchú Tum Foundation aided in the return, pressuring the government to buy fincas near the town of Xamán and turn the land over to about two hundred families of former exiles. Once the settlers moved to the land, the foundation provided seeds for crops and helped develop educational and health care facilities in the region. Within a year, the work was so successful in Xamán that outside observers were planning to use it as a model for establishing other cooperative settlements for returning refugees worldwide.

Returning Home Once Again

While Menchú was involved in intense negotiations concerning the Xamán project, she continued to receive international honors. The United Nations declared 1993 as the International Year of the Indigenous Peoples, and appointed Menchú goodwill ambassador for the year. It designated 1994–2003 as the International Decade of Indigenous Peoples and named Menchú the official spokeswoman for the decade. When this honor was bestowed on Menchú in Paris, UN director-general Federico Mayor thanked the Nobel laureate for "her efforts on behalf of ethnic minorities and indigenous peoples" and stated Rigoberta Menchú "is the culture of peace."[55]

As a symbol of the quest for peace, Menchú made a difficult decision to return to Guatemala in January 1994 after thirteen years in exile. She not only felt that she could be more instrumental in working for peace if she lived in her native land, but she also longed to be reunited with surviving members of her family. Around the time of her move, Menchú began her own family when she and companion Angel Francisco Canil Grave adopted an infant, Mash Nawalja, whose name means "spirit of water." Soon after the adoption, Canil Grave and Menchú were married.

Even as Menchú's life was changing, so was the destiny of Guatemala. The United Nations was moderating peace talks between the government and the guerrillas, who were now united under the organization Guatemalan National Revolutionary Unity (URNG). As part of the agreement, the UN established the Commission for Historical Clarification (CEH). According to the organization's Web site, the CEH was founded to "clarify with all objectivity, equity and impartiality the human rights violations and acts of violence that have caused the Guatemalan population to suffer, connected with the armed conflict. . . [and to formulate] specific recommendations to encourage peace and national harmony in Guatemala."[56]

Massacre in Xamán

Despite the steps toward reconciliation, the violence continued in Guatemala, and some of it was aimed directly at Menchú's most successful project. On October 5, 1995, settlers in Xamán were preparing a huge fiesta to celebrate the first anniversary of their settlement. As children were leaving school in the afternoon, about twenty-five heavily armed soldiers entered the town. Although the soldiers claimed they only wanted to participate in the fiesta, their presence alarmed the settlers. A crowd of about 250 people gathered in the town square and began yelling at the military men. Village elders stepped in and ordered the soldiers to leave, warning them that they were in violation of the UN accord. The soldiers, possibly motivated by panic, opened fire and threw several hand grenades into the crowd. A total of nine adults and two children were killed and another thirty people were wounded, some severely.

When Menchú learned of the massacre, she traveled to Xamán to comfort the wounded and to listen to terrifying stories from the survivors. In the years that followed, she took part in an effort to

Menchú weds longtime companion Angel Francisco Canil Grave in a 1998 ceremony in Guatemala.

bring the soldiers to justice in the Guatemalan courts, the first such case in the nation's history. The case dragged on for years.

Peace with Problems

When the Xamán massacre occurred, Menchú was working to register voters for the upcoming 1996 election. The favored candidate was Guatemala City mayor Alvaro Arzú, a reformer whom Menchú supported. After Arzú won with 70 percent of the national vote, Menchú began collaborating with his administration to broker a final peace agreement between the government and the guerrillas. With Menchú's influence, the agreement also included explicit recognition of indigenous rights.

On December 29, 1996, church bells rang and citizens lit candles to celebrate the signing of the final UN-brokered agreement, called "Accord for Firm and Lasting Peace." The accord, which ended thirty-six years of conflict, called for the demobilization of two hundred thousand paramilitary troops and the reemployment and resettling of about three thousand resistance fighters. The agreement was strongly supported by the United States, which committed $400 million to fund the implementation of the pact.

The end of war did not signal the beginning of peace and prosperity in Guatemala, however. Arzú purged the government of military officers associated with the civil war, but human rights workers, journalists, union organizers, and indigenous rights activists continued to face extreme violence. Many of these political crimes were perpetrated by unemployed former members of government death squads. Some of these people also turned to kidnapping, drug trafficking, and auto theft to support themselves after the war.

"The Same as Before"

The peace accord between the military and the guerrillas in Guatemala ended a thirty-six-year-long civil war. However, as indigenous farmer Ignacio Bizarro Ujpán writes in *Joseño*, the peace treaty did little to change the life of the average Guatemalan:

It has been a year and seven months since the peace treaty was signed by those in power, but we poor people and Indians are the same as before—marginalized, forgotten, and despised. Every day prices go up; fertilizers cost more. There is no way the poor can help themselves. The big millionaires get richer, while the poor continue in extreme poverty. In the peace negotiations, they talked about equality for all Guatemalans and the distribution of land. All of this was a lie. The lands that truly belong to the Guatemalans are in the hands of the big landowners, who are aligned with the government. The poor people still end up in extreme poverty. . . .

It was heard that after the peace accords were signed, the developed countries gave a lot of money to change the image of the country. The truth is that this money ended up in the pockets of the wolves, [because there is] much corruption in Guatemala. They spend a little of the money on the infrastructure of the towns and the rest [goes] in their pockets.

Ignacio Bizarro Ujpán, *Joseño*. Albuquerque: University of New Mexico Press, 2001, p. 256.

Guatemala Never Again

Government-sponsored violence was in the news once again on April 24, 1998, when Bishop Juan Gerardi Conedera released the report *Guatemala Never Again* as part of the Catholic Church's Recovery of Historical Memory (REMHI) project. The report contained explicit details concerning the Guatemalan army's role in the civil war and blamed 90 percent of human rights violations on government forces. In a stunning reminder that some of those forces were still active, Gerardi Conedera was beaten to death two days after the report was released.

Despite Gerardi's murder, the REMHI project played an extremely important role in Guatemala, as Menchú explains in an interview with Jo-Marie Burt and Fred Rosen in *NACLA Report on the Americas* magazine:

> [The] REMHI was designed to be a participatory investigation, in which community leaders—many of whom were Mayan—interviewed over 6,000 victims and eyewitnesses. This made it possible to collect information about more than 50,000 cases of human rights violations, and out of these individual memories to begin to construct a collective memory. . . . It marks the first time in our history that indigenous people were active participants in the writing of their own history. And they were also participants in drawing up the recommendations for the future to ensure that these atrocities never happen again. It was also a small compensation to the victims for all they had suffered—for the first time they could tell their stories without fear and be certain that it was not in vain.[57]

Controversy over *I, Rigoberta Menchú*

In 1998, even as reconciliation was coming to Guatemala, Menchú herself became a target of controversy following the release of David Stoll's book *Rigoberta Menchú and the Story of All Poor Guatemalans.* Stoll alleges that *I, Rigoberta Menchú* contains a number of inaccuracies and exaggerations. For example, the author says Menchú was not an eyewitness to her brother's murder and that her father was not a political organizer of rebel groups. Stoll also maintains that Menchú received an education through seventh grade at a boarding school run by Catholic nuns and that she was taught Spanish at this school. This would have taken place when Menchú claimed she was laboring on coffee plantations eight months a year. Responding to this last allegation, Menchú says that she did not attend the school, run by Belgian nuns, but worked as a servant there, mopping floors and cleaning toilets. Concerning the overall tone of Stoll's book, Menchú told journalists Jo-Marie Burt and Fred Rosen:

> In many ways, during the 1980s, I was a solitary indigenous voice, the only survivor, upon whom fell the task of traveling the world, going to the UN and to human rights groups around the world to tell them of what was

Thousands fill Guatemala City's central plaza for a funeral mass on the first anniversary of the slaying of Bishop Juan Gerardi Conedera.

happening in Guatemala. Now there is an effort to say that this solitary voice is not valid. But this is not the 1980s, when people were silent and there were many reasons to worry; now we are over 30,000 strong, and every story being told, every testimony gathered by REMHI and the UN Commission, is part of the broader tapestry of thousands of stories that are being woven together to write our history. . . . The implication of the charges is that if Rigoberta Menchú—the best-known Indian from Guatemala, a Nobel laureate—is lying, then these Indians who are unknown must also be lying. We believe there is a malicious element in all of this, and, moreover, that it is politically motivated. We are unsure where this political campaign is coming from. But we have no doubt that there are sectors who do not want the people to tell their stories.[58]

Stoll's reaction to this defense remains unknown. Although he does concede that the Guatemalan army committed countless atrocities, he accuses Menchú of alleging that what happened to others actually happened to her. Those who defend Menchú point out that she is speaking from what is called collective memory, common among indigenous people and other repressed groups. As Stoll explains this term, it means "since she is speaking for her people, it is not very important whether the experiences she describes actually happened to her, or whether they happened exactly the way she says, because they represent the collective experience of the Mayas."[59]

Whatever the criticism of I, Rigoberta Menchú, it is undisputed that both of Menchú's parents and her brother Petrocinio died horrible deaths because of their political actions, and it is well documented that about two hundred thousand Mayans suffered similar fates. Thus Menchú's story is the story of all indigenous Guatemalans in the 1970s and 1980s, as book reviewer S. McClure writes:

Books of this type are ultimately intended to create awareness. They can either be the narcissistic autobiography that only chronicles the achievements of an individual person, or first-person narrative books, like Menchú's, that attempt to illustrate the lifestyle of a certain class of people. They are used as tools to further a cause, uphold or change a certain doctrine, or chronicle events in a person or culture's life. Menchú's book is both credible and authentic because it succeeds in bringing the plight of the Guatemalan poor into the forefront using events that are factual, if not personal. . . . Literature like hers is important for all of humanity because without her voice it becomes much more difficult for other societies to respond and attempt to vindicate those who have been victimized by oppressive and nefarious regimes. Thus, it is the message that is far more important for humanity's sake than the futile squabbling over gratuitous details that have no real ramifications on the overall outcome of the people who are being oppressed.[60]

Human Dignity

[This] Maya woman turned out not to accept her lot and then sinned by becoming a universal symbol of human dignity, oh my God. Powerful men in Guatemala and in the world hate that.

Eduardo Galeano, "Let's Shoot Rigoberta Menchú," *La Jomada*, January 16, 1999, p. 6.

While the debate over her first book raged, Menchú released her second book, *Crossing Borders*, in 1998. The following year a report was released by Guatemala's Truth and Reconciliation Commission, also known as the Commission for Historical Clarification (CEH). This report, *Memory of Silence*, fulfilled a mandate of the UN-brokered peace accord to investigate human rights abuses on both sides of the civil war. The CEH found that the army and the government-sponsored Civilian Civil Self-Defense Patrols were responsible for 92 percent of the arbitrary executions and 91 percent of "forced disappearances." Eighty-three percent of the victims were indigenous Maya. The guerrilla groups were held responsible for 3 percent of the human rights abuses, including 5 percent of the arbi-

Menchú, shown here in native garb, sued the Guatemalan government for genocide in a Spanish court in 2000.

trary executions and 2 percent of forced disappearances. Ninety-one percent of the violations occurred between 1978 and 1984.

Filing Charges

In December 2000 Menchú used evidence provided by the *Memory of Silence* report to file charges of genocide in the Spanish National Court (SNC) in Madrid against three

Guatemalan presidents. Although Spain does not have jurisdiction over Guatemala, a 1985 Spanish law gives the SNC jurisdiction over cases related to international crimes regardless of the nationality of the perpetrator or where the crime took place. These crimes, such as genocide, terrorism, and piracy, are considered so egregious that they are looked upon as offenses against the entire world. In addition, Spanish law allows ordinary citizens, not just government prosecutors, to pursue criminal actions by filing criminal complaints.

In filing her case, Menchú based her charges on three specific incidents: the military assault on the Spanish embassy in 1980 in which her father died along with thirty-five others, the murder of four Spanish priests who were sympathetic to the indigenous cause, and the torture and murder of Menchú's mother and brother. In Guatemala, members of the military responded by formally filing charges against Menchú for treason. Because of these charges and

Menchú waves to well-wishers after voting in 2003. She remains dedicated to indigenous rights, especially for her beloved Maya.

continuing death threats, Menchú was forced into exile for the third time, moving back to Mexico City in 2001.

As the case wound its way through the Spanish justice system over the course of several years, Menchú continued with her writing career. Wishing to publish a positive recollection of her life, she wrote a children's book, *The Girl from Chimel*, vividly illustrated by the Mexican artist Domi. In the book, Menchú recalls happy childhood memories of her grandfather, the forest, the cornfields, and the sacred mountains. Like her other books, *The Girl from Chimel* was received with widespread critical acclaim. The book was translated into English in 2005.

My Commitment Knows No Boundaries or Limits

Menchú's exile ended once again in 2004 when Guatemala's new president, Oscar Berger, invited her to come home and join his administration. Berger appointed Menchú as the goodwill ambassador to the 1996 UN-brokered peace accords so she could monitor the Guatemalan government's adherence to the agreement. This new position would have been beyond the imagination of the little girl from Chimel who labored twelve hours a day in deplorable conditions.

Today, Menchú remains dedicated to indigenous rights and to the Maya people. The final words of *I, Rigoberta Menchú*, written when she was only twenty-two years old, continue to shed light on her motivations:

> [My cause] wasn't born out of something good, it was born out of wretchedness and bitterness. It has been radicalized by the poverty in which my people live. It has been radicalized by the malnutrition which I, as an Indian, have seen and experienced. And by the exploitation and discrimination which I've felt in the flesh. And by the oppression which prevents us performing our ceremonies, and shows no respect for our way of life, the way we are. At the same time, they've killed the people dearest to me   . Therefore, my commitment to our struggle knows no boundaries or limits.[61]

Notes

Introduction: A Struggle to Survive

1. Angharad N. Valdivia, *A Latina in the Land of Hollywood.* Tucson: University of Arizona Press, 2000, p. 111.
2. T. Patrick Culbert, *Maya Civilization.* Washington, DC: Smithsonian Books, 1993, p. 19.
3. Quoted in James Painter, *Guatemala: False Hope False Freedom.* London: Catholic Institute for International Relations, 1987, p. 14.
4. Larry Habegger and Natanya Pearlman, *Travelers' Tales Central America.* San Francisco: Travelers' Tales, 2002, p. 206.

Chapter 1: The Story of Poor Guatemalans

5. Global Exchange, "Guatemala: A Brief History." December 1, 2004. www.globalexchange.org/countries/americas/guatemala/history.htm.
6. Global Exchange, "Guatemala: A Brief History."
7. Quoted in Stephen Schlesinger and Stephen Kinzer, *Bitter Fruit: The Story of the American Coup in Guatemala.* Cambridge, MA: Harvard University, David Rockefeller Center for Latin American Studies, 1999, p. 246.
8. Rigoberta Menchú, *I, Rigoberta Menchú: An Indian Woman in Guatemala,* ed. Elisabeth Burgos, trans. *Ann Wright.* London: Verso, 1984, p. 2.
9. Quoted in David Stoll, *Rigoberta Menchú and the Story of All Poor Guatemalans.* Boulder, CO: Westview, 1998, p. 29.
10. Menchú, *I, Rigoberta Menchú,* pp. 21–22.
11. Menchú, *I, Rigoberta Menchú,* p. 4.
12. Menchú, *I, Rigoberta Menchú,* p. 23.
13. Quoted in Stoll, *Rigoberta Menchú,* p. 32.
14. Menchú, *I, Rigoberta Menchú,* p. 104.
15. Menchú, *I, Rigoberta Menchú,* p. 106.
16. Quoted in Menchú, *I, Rigoberta Menchú,* p. 109.

Chapter 2: A Young Activist

17. Victor Perera, *Unfinished Conquest.* Berkeley and Los

Angeles: University of California Press, 1993, pp. 41–42.

18. Menchú, *I, Rigoberta Menchú*, pp. 122–23.
19. Quoted in Stoll, *Rigoberta Menchú*, p. 89.
20. Stoll, *Rigoberta Menchú*, p. 90.
21. Greg Grandin, "An Interview with Greg Grandin," University of Chicago Press, 2004. www.press.uchicago. edu/Misc/Chicago/305724in.html.
22. Menchú, *I, Rigoberta Menchú*, p. 160.
23. Menchú, *I, Rigoberta Menchú*, pp. 165–66.
24. Menchú, *I, Rigoberta Menchú*, p. 167.
25. Quoted in Stoll, *Rigoberta Menchú*, p. 98.
26. Perera, *Unfinished Conquest*, p. 69.
27. Perera, *Unfinished Conquest*, p. 68.
28. Menchú, *I, Rigoberta Menchú*, p. 177.
29. Perera, *Unfinished Conquest*, p. 106.

Chapter 3: Escape from Guatemala
30. Stoll, *Rigoberta Menchú*, p. 71.
31. Stoll, *Rigoberta Menchú*, pp. 71–72.
32. Quoted in Harry Fried, "Popular Front Grows in Guatemala,"*New York Guardian*, August 19, 1981, p. 13.
33. Menchú, *I, Rigoberta Menchú*, p. 203.
34. Menchú, *I, Rigoberta Menchú*, pp. 231–32.
35. Rigoberta Menchú, *Crossing Borders*. New York: Verso, 1998, pp. 97–98.
36. Menchú, *Crossing Borders*, p. 107.

Chapter 4: Telling Her Story to the World
37. Menchú, *Crossing Borders*, p. 113.
38. Menchú, *I, Rigoberta Menchú*, pp. xiv–xv.
39. Menchú, *I, Rigoberta Menchú*, pp. xx.
40. Menchú, *Crossing Borders*, p. 114.
41. Eric DC, "When the Mountains Tremble," review, amazon.com, September 8, 2005. www.amazon.com/ gp/product/B0002HOD7W/qid=1152383047/sr=8-1/ref =pd_bbs_1/002-3831263-4156060?n=507846&s=dvd&v =glance.
42. International Indian Treaty Council, "Our Mission," 2006. www.treatycouncil.org/home.htm.

43. Menchú, *Crossing Borders*, p. 124.
44. Menchú, *Crossing Borders*, pp. 129–30.
45. Stoll, *Rigoberta Menchú*, p. 205.
46. Quoted in Painter, *Guatemala: False Hope False Freedom*, p. x.
47. Menchú, *Crossing Borders*, p. 2.
48. Menchú, *Crossing Borders*, p. 168.

Chapter 5: The Nobel Laureate
49. Menchú, *Crossing Borders*, p. 2.
50. Stoll, *Rigoberta Menchú*, p. 211.
51. Quoted in Menchú, *Crossing Borders*, p. 10.
52. Quoted in Tim Golden, "Guatemala Indian Wins the Nobel Peace Prize," *New York Times*, October 17, 1992, p. 1.
53. Quoted in Valdivia, *A Latina in the Land of Hollywood*, p.118.
54. Quoted in Glenn Welker, "Homage to Rigoberta Menchú Tum, Quiché Mayan," Indians.org, October 3, 1998. www.indians.org/welker/Menchú.htm.
55. Quoted in "UNESCO Names Rigoberta Menchú Tum Goodwill Ambassador for Culture of Peace," UNESCO.org, June 21, 1993. www.unesco.org/op/eng/unescopress/96-127e.htm.
56. Conciliation Resources, "Commission for Historical Clarification Accord," 2005. www.c-r.org/accord/guat/accord2/hist_cla.shtml.
57. Jo-Marie Burt and Fred Rosen, "Truth-Telling and Memory in Postwar Guatemala: An Interview with Rigoberta Menchú," *NACLA Report on the Americas*, March/April 1999, p. 6.
58. Burt and Rosen, "Truth-Telling and Memory in Postwar Guatemala," p. 6.
59. Stoll, *Rigoberta Menchú*, p. 190.
60. S. McClure, "A Credible and Important Piece of Literature," review, Amazon.com, December 15, 2005. www.amazon.com /gp/product/0860917886/qid=1152039643/sr=8-1/ref=pd_bbs_1/002-5214228-4143205?n=507846&s=books&v =glance.
61. Menchú, *I, Rigoberta Menchú*, pp. 246–47.

Important Dates

1959

January 9: Rigoberta Menchú is born in Guatemala.

1970

September 29: Rigoberta's father, Vicente Menchú, is arrested for the first time in a dispute over land.

1977

September: Vicente Menchú is arrested again and held for fifteen days.

1978

Vicente Menchú helps found the Committee for Peasant Unity (CUC).

1979

September 9: Rigoberta's brother Petrocinio is captured by military authorities, tortured for sixteen days, and burned to death in front of family members.

1980

January 31: Vicente Menchú is killed in a suspicious fire after helping take over the Spanish embassy in Guatemala City.
April 9: Rigoberta's mother, Juana, is captured, tortured, and killed by the Guatemalan military.

Rigoberta Menchú joins the January 31st Popular Front, a group of united guerrillas, student groups, and peasant organizations. Menchú goes into exile for the first time in Chiapas, Mexico.

1982

January: Menchú tells the story of her life to Elisabeth Burgos in Paris. Her narrative is turned into the book *I, Rigoberta Menchú: An Indian Woman in Guatemala*.

1984

When the Mountains Tremble, a film about the ongoing civil war in Guatemala and featuring Menchú, is released.

1982–1992

Menchú works through the United Nations to promote the cause of indigenous rights in Guatemala and elsewhere.

1992

Menchú wins the Nobel Peace Prize.

1996

December 29: A UN-brokered peace accord officially ends the Guatemalan civil war after thirty-six years.

1998

Menchú's second book, *Crossing Borders*, is published.

2000

Menchú's children's book, *Girl from Chimel*, is published.

2004

Menchú is invited by Guatemala's new president, Oscar Berger, to work with the government to monitor Guatemala's adherence to the peace accord.

For More Information

Books

Marlene Targ Brill, *Journey for Peace: The Story of Rigoberta Menchú*. New York: Dutton, 1996. A biography of Rigoberta Menchú that covers the period between her childhood in rural Guatemala and her winning of the Nobel Peace Prize.

Alexander Ewen, *Voices of Indigenous People*. Santa Fe, NM: Clear Light, 1994. Published for the UN International Year of the World's Indigenous People, this book contains messages from nineteen indigenous leaders and a foreword by Rigoberta Menchú.

Rigoberta Menchú, *The Girl from Chimel*. Toronto: Groundwood, 2005. A richly illustrated book in which the author recalls happy memories of her childhood in a small Guatemalan village.

————, *I, Rigoberta Menchú: An Indian Woman in Guatemala*. Ed. Elisabeth Burgos. Trans. Ann Wright. London: Verso, 1984. The autobiographical account of Guatemala's most famous indigenous citizen, with details of the author's early life, her role in the civil war, and the deaths of her family members.

Marion Morrison, *Guatemala*. New York: Children's, 2005. An exploration of Guatemala's natural wonders, ancient societies, modern problems, and vibrant culture.

Web Sites

Foundation for Human Rights in Guatemala
(www.fhrg.org/mambo/index.php). The latest news from Guatemala concerning human rights abuses, trials of former government officials, and planned protests and demonstrations.

Guatemala (http://lanic.utexas.edu/la/ca/guatemala). A Web site hosted by the Latin American Network Information Center, with links to dozens of sites concerning academics and research, arts and culture, business and economy, magazines, news, organizations, government, politics, and human rights.

Guatemala Human Rights Commission/USA (www.ghrc-usa.org). A Web site hosted by a humanitarian organization founded in 1982 to monitor, document, and report on the human rights situation in Guatemala.

Guatemala Post (www.guatemaladaily.com). An online newspaper with news about Guatemalan politics, sports, business, and entertainment, along with links to Guatemalan radio stations.

Revue Magazine (www.revuemag.com). Guatemala's English-language magazine with El Salvador, Honduras, and Belize sections.

Rigoberta Menchú Tum: The Nobel Peace Prize 1992: Nobel Lecture (http://nobelprize.org/nobel_prizes/peace/laureates/1992/tum-lecture.html). A Web site with the full acceptance speech Menchú gave upon receiving the Nobel Peace Prize.

DVD

Peter Kinoy, Pamela Yates, Thomas Sigel, *When the Mountains Tremble*, docudrama, 2004. This twentieth anniversary DVD edition of the documentary originally released in 1983 chronicles the painful life story of Nobel Prize winner Rigoberta Menchú and documents the violence between the heavily armed Guatemalan military personnel and the nearly defenseless Maya population.

Index

Picture Credits

About the Author

Stuart A. Kallen is the author of more than two hundred nonfiction books for children and young adults. He has written on topics ranging from the theory of relativity to the history of rock and roll. In addition, Mr. Kallen has written award-winning children's videos and television scripts. In his spare time, Kallen is a singer/songwriter/guitarist in San Diego, California.